The Dog Whisperer

the Dog Whisperer

The essential guide to understanding and raising a happy dog

**John Richardson &
Leslye Sharon Cole**

NEW
HOLLAND

First published in Australia in 2001 by
New Holland Publishers (Australia) Pty Ltd
Sydney · Auckland · London · Cape Town

14 Aquatic Drive Frenchs Forest NSW 2086 Australia
218 Lake Road Northcote Auckland New Zealand
86 Edgware Road London W2 2EA United Kingdom
80 McKenzie Street Cape Town 8001 South Africa

10 9 8 7 6 5

National Library of Australia Cataloguing-in-Publication Data:

Richardson, John May 1944–.
The dog whisperer: the essential guide to understanding and raising a happy dog
Includes index.
ISBN 1 86436 698 2
1. Dogs—Training. 2. Dogs—Behaviour. I. Cole, Leslye. II. Title

636.70887

Publishing Manager: Anouska Good
Senior Editor: Monica Ban
Designer: Nanette Backhouse
Production: Pica
Printer: Times

This book was typeset in Marathon Light 10.5pt

The author and publisher have made every effort to ensure the information contained in this
book was correct at the time of going to press and accept no responsibility for any loss, injury
or inconvenience sustained by any person using this book.

You can contact Dogtech on (02) 9772 2861 or visit their website at www.dogtech.com.au

Contents

3. Putting the Keys into Practice · 73

4. Training Techniques · 97

Dedication

I dedicate this book to my wife, Hazel, in love and appreciation for her help and support with this book.

I would also like to mention the other important people in my life— my parents, Ed and Lil; my sisters, Doreen and Sylvia, for the camaraderie we had whilst growing up; and my daughters, Michele and Kelly, who share my love of dogs.

Acknowledgements

There are many people to whom I am indebted for their assistance during the writing of this book. In particular, I wish to thank Leslye Sharon Cole for her illustrations; Lorraine Hamilton for the foreword; Dr David Ball, B.V.Sc., M.Sc., Dip.Ed, for his input on dietary aspects; Inspector Commander Peter Crumblin for inviting me to the Police Dog Unit at Menai; Sgt. Paul Doney, Training Co-ordinator, for passing on his knowledge of how the Unit works and what skills are required by both dog and handler to become an effective team; and to Senior Constable Matt McCaldie and 'Merlin' for demonstrating those skills. I would also like to thank Jenny Judson for her help and guidance; Susan and Ray Pitstock; The Greyhound Adoption Program (NSW) Inc; Ron Arnold and Alan Batchelor of Harold Park; Shane Clarke of Pestforce and 'Alf'; Jim Silver and King; the owners of Boss; and the Siberian Husky and Alaskan Malamute Club of South Australia Inc.

Leslye would like to thank John and Hazel Richardson for the opportunity to illustrate this book; Anouska Good, Monica Ban and Nanette Backhouse at New Holland; and the following people for their help and support: Rod Cole, Tim and Tessa Cole, Max and Elaine Coates, Monty Sloane, Jim Brandenburg, Brodee Myers-Cooke, Rod and Rai Schieb, and Garry and Susie Murphie.

Foreword

In my ten years of experience, culminating in the management of an animal shelter, I have been appalled at the number of dogs surrendered by owners due solely to problems occurring as the result of a lack of training. A large number of these dogs have died needlessly, and had their owners had a better understanding of the thought processes of a dog, many of them may have been saved from such a fate.

Amongst the many stories I have heard, one springs to mind. The case of a small, seemingly happy dog who had bitten on several occasions, and when seated comfortably on the lounge, would not allow anyone to remove him. He obviously believed that he was where he had a right to be, according to his own understanding of his position in the household. Right from the start, the little fellow had been treated as a 'woolly human' (to use John's terminology). The matter may well have been resolved quickly and easily, using John's training methods, had the owner understood why the dog was acting in such a way. That little dog was one of many unfortunate animals to lose its life, due more to human error than any fault of its own.

I have always believed that to be a successful part of a family, a dog needs to have good manners, according to our human standards. Over the years, I had seen different styles of dog training, but was still to have my eyes opened to the more gentle reward-based methods of communicating our desires to our dogs.

I first saw John work his magic at a seminar, where he demonstrated his skills with two energetic, young working breed dogs, borrowed from the shelter. Both dogs had been surrendered to the shelter because they had outgrown their 'cute' stage, and had entered the inevitable difficult 'teenage' period of their lives. They were a handful and their owners did not have the knowledge, nor the desire, to deal with this. I was impressed at how quickly and effortlessly John put his theories into practice, and how within a very short time each dog was calm and concentrating solely on him, in spite of the obvious distractions of a crowd and the inevitable interesting aromas of a strange new place. The dogs seemed oblivious to everything and everyone around them, and were quickly beginning the process of a new way of learning, and clearly enjoying it. I was hooked!

Since then, I have become a dedicated advocate of this gentle, intelligent method of communicating with our dogs. If all dog owners had the knowledge and understanding to use such simple, humane methods, I feel sure that the shelters and pounds would not be forced into the unenviable position of having to euthanase healthy young dogs, simply due to behaviour mismanagement.

John is spreading his word as much as possible. As the founder of DogTech International and his individual in-home behavioural modification sessions, as well as his work in training veterinary nurses, and as a Canine Good Citizens Instructor, he is opening the eyes of other people involved with dogs. He conducts seminars and workshops to help staff and inspectors of shelters and pounds understand how to deal with aggression in some of the dogs they are confronted with. For such people, having the knowledge to interpret the body language displayed by a dog may indeed prevent a dangerous situation from escalating into an attack.

With this book, John will be able to reach even more people involved with dogs. Readers will gain an understanding of the dog psyche, and why different breeds have different characteristics. I find it exciting that as a result of reading John's book, even more people will come to use positive, motivational, reward-based training methods. It can only be good for all dog-kind.

Lorraine Hamilton
Animal Shelter Manager, A.C.T.
April 2001

My Mate Monty

by John Richardson

England in winter can be a very exciting place when you are six years of age and have just been given your first dog. As a child growing up in this cold climate, I would often wake up early in winter, when it had been snowing, to build a snowman and take my dog Monty outside to play. I would throw snowballs for him to fetch, which was one of our favourite games. Monty would run after the frozen balls, but could rarely find them as they would usually disintegrate as they hit the ground. When the snow was icy, and the snowballs didn't break up, he would find it difficult to hold the icy snowballs in his mouth. But with all this, he still loved the game and, of course, so did I.

Monty was a little fluffy-haired four-year-old terrier that looked like a cross-Cairn terrier, although the family could never quite agree on his parentage. My parents had acquired him from our Aunt Peggy, who had decided to give the dog away because her son had somehow brought home a monkey from a trip overseas! Aunt Peggy had said that the monkey would jump on Monty's back when he wasn't looking and scare him, and Monty would then become very aggressive, attacking the monkey. She told us that they were trying to tear each other apart, and that is why Monty came to live with us.

The local primary school I attended was only fifteen minutes away from home. Many days, Monty would come with me to school, but as dogs weren't allowed on the school premises, Monty and I would part at the school gate, with a few dozen pats. I never knew what he did after that but he was always excitedly waiting for me when I got home. I would say 'Hi' to Mum, grab a few biscuits for Monty and myself, and off we would go to play.

Away from the watchful eyes of my mother, I would get involved in all types of mischief, which sometimes included Monty and I chasing away boys who had called me names. In these encounters, I would chase the offenders down our lane with Monty alongside of me and, as he was the faster of us, he would catch up with the boys, run in front of them and bark until the boys had to stop. He would sometimes even pin them up against a wall until I got there—just like a sheepdog rounding up his sheep. I would then reprimand the boys for their name calling, and send them on their way.

Yes, little Johnny, at only six years of age, was definitely not mature enough to be in charge of a dog and didn't understand the possible dangers of his actions. My experience taught me a vital lesson, and this is why I feel strongly that children who have a dog need parental supervision at all times.

Being so young, I can't quite remember exactly what happened after these escapades, but I think some of the children must have complained to their parents. I only had Monty for about six months, when one day I came home from school to be told that Monty had gone to live in the country on a farm, as the city was not a good place for an active dog like him. I cried for days and was never going to speak to my parents again. However, two weeks later my Mum bought me a little white rabbit—so a bit of the hurt went away.

Many years later, my mother told me the truth. Neighbours had complained that Monty had been bailing them up and they were afraid that one of their children may be bitten, so my parents, being the responsible people they were, had decided that Monty had to go. They had actually sent him off to the local shelter.

As part of the many engagements I have with dogs these days, one of the things I enjoy the most is the voluntary work I do with shelter dogs, which may be because of this unfortunate experience I had early in my own life. I never found out what became of Monty. I really don't know if Monty was 'put down' or if he ended up being adopted by a kind person in the country who would play catch using snowballs, the way I did with him—but I hope this is what happened to my little mate.

As an Australian Standards Accredited Instructor, Canine Good Citizens Accredited Instructor and lecturer of Canine Behaviour at Sydney Technical College, I advise and assist local government and animal welfare shelters in dog behaviour problems. I would like to share with you my experiences, ideas and the knowledge that I have learnt up to now, so that dog owners everywhere can fully understand how to effectively interact with their four-legged friends.

In this book I will introduce you to Whisper Wise motivational training, a system of non-aggressive, positive reinforcement dog training which not only uses the ways of the wolf as a guide but also combines psychological, physical and emotional aspects of our dogs.

This technique has been developed by me through thirty years of dog training—from winning ribbons at obedience trials with my German shepherds, to the accomplishments of my company DogTech International which is one of the most successful in-home dog training companies operating in Australia today.

You can now use Whisper Wise effectively on your dog, just as I have done with the dogs of countless happy clients, to eliminate the sort of bad behaviour mentioned above.

In better understanding dogs, hopefully in time we humans will not have to keep destroying the ones that we say we love!

Introduction

by Leslye Sharon Cole

How many times have you heard a dog owner say, 'My dog thinks it's a person'. In our desire to personify man's best friend we make one very big mistake—our dog does not actually think it is one of us. In its canine mind it thinks that we are a part of its family. It sees us as members of its pack.

I was first introduced to this way of thinking while watching John Richardson on a television appearance for 'A Current Affair', early in 1999, where he was announced as The Dog Whisperer. I was amazed as he tamed a barking, unruly dog with such gentleness and understanding, talking to it throughout the segment only with whispers. His success in solving the problem so quickly convinced me that he must be psychic, with the ability to communicate with dogs just by using his mind!

This may not have actually been true, but nevertheless, he was the first person we called when our family was having behavioural problems with our gorgeous Doberman, Sapphie.

As she was approaching eighteen months of age, the protective guard dog instinct in her became so strong that we were having trouble with her when anyone came near the house. This is not very convenient when you work at home relying on couriers to deliver clients' briefs and despatch artwork (sometimes many times a day), as I do. Eventually, I ended up in tears after Sapphie nearly took a chunk out of my agent's hand. She was also pulling us all around the neighbourhood when she was taking us for a walk.

John was booked out, of course, so we waited patiently for four weeks until our appointment. On arriving, he had plenty of questions and warned us that his methods were rather unconventional. I'll say they were unconventional! To my horror, instead of watching him do his magic, John did not even want to see the dog until after he had given my husband and I a one-hour talk on what dogs are all about. John explained to us about how dogs fit into the family and the instinctive nature of the way domestic dogs think. He only needed to see Sapphie for about five minutes to assess her emotional state and see how aggressive she was with a stranger in the house. I wanted to see the whispering. Then we were given our homework, starting off with a few of the techniques outlined in this book—mainly relating to dominance.

Needless to say, we followed through with the advice and to our amazement, her behaviour was improving. John gave us some simple solutions for when a courier or guest called in, which worked beautifully. Instead of dreading a knock at the door, I could relax, knowing I had a method that would not upset Sapphie, or the person on the other side of the door.

After two more visits, where we did see John work his magic, Sapphie was virtually a different dog. We could even take her for an enjoyable walk, this time with our obedient dog walking calmly, close to our side and with a slack lead!

His work with Sapphie, and us, led to a creative association I am sincerely grateful for, culminating in our first book together. It has been a pleasure to work with John, to learn more about these beautiful animals, and illustrating his original theories. My thanks also go out to Monty Sloan who can be visited at www.wolfpark.org (look for his chronicles on a wolf called Orca), and Jim Brandenburg for the incredible wolf photos I marvelled at while gathering my references. Studying the magnificent wolves has given me a new understanding of them and our domestic dogs.

In this book, John Richardson shows us how being aware of the fact that your dog thinks that we are part of its pack, can help us to understand why dogs behave as they do and why this rationale forms the basis of his unique training method.

John also relates a wealth of information on all aspects of a dog's life, including ten essential steps to help us retrain our dogs and ourselves. Clear instructions and actual case studies demonstrate how his, sometimes controversial, methods are put into practice with great success.

It serves as the ultimate guide to dog owners everywhere who want to understand their canine companion better and put an end to their bad behaviour.

The Ways of the Wolf

The wolf (*Canis lupus*) has existed in many parts of the world for hundreds of thousands of years. The earliest remains from North America are dated at approximately 700 000 years old. These mysterious creatures have been feared by many and superstition has surrounded them in strange tales depicting the wolf as a calculating and vicious killer. In early times, the church used the example of the wolf preying on defenceless lambs as a metaphor for the presence of the Devil amongst us. Stories have circulated for centuries about humans transforming into wolf-like creatures that roam to savage and kill people—monsters that we call werewolves. Movies of this subject persist in perpetuating the myth. Then there was poor Little Red Riding Hood who had all that trouble with the Wicked Wolf posing as her grandmother! Many fairy stories told to children all over the world talk about the Big Bad Wolf. Just think of those Three Little Pigs and Peter, who even managed to defeat this villain. It is no wonder many people have an irrational fear and dislike for wolves. For as we know, little knowledge of a subject can be misleading, and very few people really know much about these majestic animals.

Even so, wolves may be more familiar than we originally might have thought. Our domestic dog (*Canis familiaris*) is a direct descendent of the wolf. The character traits that endear the dog to us—courage, intelligence and loyalty—are the very same characteristics that the wolf needs to survive in the wild. Using their acute senses, they have the ability to interpret what is happening in their environment with a subtlety we have no hope of understanding. Their hunting skills were so admired by the natives of North America that they called it 'The Teacher'. The wolf was honoured in their ceremonies and dances.

Although wolves became our fiercest enemy, domestic dogs became 'man's best friend'. Through selective breeding, we have been able to change the physical appearance of the dog enormously from that of its ancestor. This difference could not be more evident than when we compare the appearance of a chihuahua with a silver wolf. However, even though we have been able to alter the way a dog looks on the outside, the dog has inherited the mind of the wolf. The domestic dog has the same instincts and chromosomes as the wolf.

I believe we must concentrate on the similarities in dog and wolf behaviour to understand our 'best friends' better. Behaviour that sometimes mystifies us, can be traced back to the natural instincts of wolves in a pack situation. Once this is understood, problems can be remedied with simple, practical steps that simulate how the wolves themselves would act in their natural environment.

Pack Animal Culture

The social structure of the wolf revolves around a group that we call a pack. The size of the pack can vary from two to approximately twelve individuals. This is usually determined by the size of prey available in the surrounding environment. The interaction between individuals is complex and in accordance with a strict hierarchy or 'pecking order'. This hierarchy places the strongest male, the alpha male, at the top, with his mate, the alpha female. The other members follow in descending order of dominance with the second in charge, the third in charge, etc., right down to the very least dominant member of the pack.

The positions in a pack are constantly changing as younger wolves challenge their superiors whenever the opportunity arises. Movement happens in the hierarchy through the display of dominance and submission. The strongest wolf will always be more dominant over the weaker wolf, which is forced into submission during a confrontation.

There are great advantages in working together in a pack situation. Wolves can understand each other's intention with such an extraordinary degree of intuition, that it seems inexplicable. Pack members instinctively coordinate the main activities such as resting, sleeping and hunting. Younger members learn from the older, more experienced members and the whole group functions as a unified and highly skilled team. Like us, they are very social animals and prefer to have their pack members around them at all times.

All members participate in hunting for food with the exception of the very young, elderly or mothers about to have puppies. The higher the number that participate in the hunt, the more efficient they will be. This pack system is also useful when there is a new addition of pups. When they are very young, the mother must spend most of her time with her offspring, relying on the other wolves to provide food for her and the litter. As the pups grow older another wolf can be assigned as 'baby-sitter' to look after the pups when the mother resumes her hunting duty.

Of course, there is also safety in numbers.

Wolf Feeding Habits

Wolves are mainly carnivorous, using their intelligence and capable hunting skills to provide food for the pack. The wolf's talent for coordinating each member creates the teamwork essential for hunting large prey such as caribou, moose or buffalo. With its strength, a wolf can pull down an animal ten times its own weight, but with every strike it risks its own life. An adult male can weigh up to 80 kg, which is far outweighed by a buffalo weighing one tonne.

The wolf knows it cannot outrun an adult caribou, or moose, and will not choose to chase one that is healthy. Instead, the pack moves around a herd, looking for an animal that might be vulnerable. It is for this reason that the Inuit say: although the wolf feeds on the caribou, it is the wolf that keeps the caribou strong. The Inuit believe that because the wolves weed out the sick and weak for their food, the remaining herd has stronger and healthier blood lines.

The sizing up continues as they persuade the herd to move, making the older and weaker more obvious. The first attack is a test, to decide whether to back off or build up more force. An attempt is made to isolate the chosen prey from the others in the herd to deny it the security and food it needs to survive. Over a period which may last days, the wolves' patience, determination and tenacity drains the isolated animal of its energy, both physically and mentally. After suffering such intense stress the animal is then brought down for the kill.

Wolves also prey on the young of these herding animals. In this case, when the herd is persuaded to move, the younger ones instinctively move toward the centre where they are protected by the shield of the adults. The wolves, with their incredible stamina, keep them running. Eventually one will stumble or become exhausted and fall to the ground.

Hunger creates extraordinary determination and adaptability. Some wolves have even perfected a technique for fishing when other sources of food are scarce.

In each case the alpha wolves eat first. They eat the best part of the animal and only leave the meal when they have had their fill. The other members of the pack take their turn in order of their place in the

The alpha wolves eat the best part of the animal first. The rest of the pack take their turn in order of their place in the hierarchy.

hierarchy. Any food not eaten is buried in a 'store' where it is kept for future needs, such as when game becomes scarce, or for mothers caring for young who cannot take part in the hunt. On average, an adult wolf eats between 2.5 and 6 kg of food every day. The pack will not hunt again until the hunger returns when the supply of food is completely gone.

Pack members left behind on hunting expeditions have food provided for them by the returning wolves. By licking them vigorously under the chin they trigger the wolves to regurgitate some of the partially digested food they have eaten while away hunting.

The collective welfare of the pack can sometimes be more important than the immediate needs of the individual.

Family Life

There is usually only one breeding pair in the pack and this is most likely to be the alpha wolves. Other members are stopped from breeding by the alpha pair's dominant behaviour. Unlike dogs, the female wolf comes into heat once a year, with mating taking place during the winter months. The gestation period is around sixty-three days and the average size of a litter is six pups. The female gives birth to her pups in an underground den or small cave. The entrance of the den is just large enough for one wolf to crawl into, widening further inside to cradle the mother and her young. The den is well hidden and kept spotlessly clean. The pups' faeces are licked away by the mother and food is brought to an area near the den, never taken in. The area surrounding the den becomes a playground as the pups grow older, and all of the pack use it as a home base.

The entrance of the den is just large enough for one wolf to crawl into. It is well hidden and kept spotlessly clean.

Solids are introduced to the pups at about one month when they grovel and lick their mother's face to encourage her to regurgitate food. The pups are then completely weaned by around the age of two months. At four months the youngsters are fully independent.

While the pups are not old enough to hunt they are kept in a rendezvous area away from the den. This is a carefully chosen place in a valley or low-lying area where fresh water is available and there is little chance of the youngsters straying. At times, when they are not supervised by their mother, she will organise another member of the pack to 'baby-sit' the young to protect them from predators.

As mentioned earlier, daily activities are instinctively coordinated. Wolves often become restless before a hunting expedition, leading up to a howling chorus, as if to announce their departure. The search for food can last for hours, even days, and any members of the pack left back at the den can become agitated waiting for the others to return. After the hunt they all enjoy a satisfied sleep lasting several hours.

Availability of food determines the density of the wolf population within a specific area. Their territories will be relatively small where the food is plentiful. One single pack can cover a large range with their territory extending hundreds of kilometres. The boundaries are rigorously marked and ruthlessly defended. Territory marking is done through the dispersal of their scent using urine and droppings. Any wolf that trespasses over the boundary of another pack is taking a great risk. A wolf will fight to the death to defend their precious hunting grounds.

Puppy Play

The mother wolf has the greatest influence on her pups' early development, through the maternal care she gives to her dependants. When the pups are newborn, virtually all social interaction is with her, as she is responsible for food, warmth, cleanliness and hygiene, as well as comfort, through touch. It is only after they open their eyes and ears that stimulation comes from the rest of their environment, including their litter mates. It is around this time that they start to wag their tails, to bark and growl, and by the time the pups are four weeks old, most of their communication blueprint has been developed. The primitive instincts of whining and crawling, to look for warmth and a teat,

Care-seeking behaviour includes licking the mother's muzzle, low tail wagging, yelping, pawing and following her like a shadow.

become more sophisticated. Care-seeking behaviour now includes licking the mother's muzzle under the chin, tail wagging (tail held low), jumping up, yelping, pawing, and following the mother as if they were her shadow. This is an important time for their socialisation, as the care-dependency relationship with their mother since birth gradually gives way to relationships based on dominance and submission.

For pups, the lessons of life are learnt through play. Individual characters and personalities can be seen almost from birth and are revealed while rumbling around together, with the first lessons of dominance and submission. These first lessons can go a long way to predict the future relationships within the pack. It is only through testing each other in play that the communication skills of the pups are learned, and this will continue to shape their social behaviour into adulthood. Play also creates the cohesive bonds with other pack

A pup will join in the howling chorus as soon as it is able.

members necessary for the pack to behave as a united group. Their very survival depends on it.

Many other important skills are learnt and refined through play, such as physical and mental coordination and agility, problem solving, understanding how an action can cause a sequence of events, exploration and finding out individual limitations within a safe environment. Wolves continue to enjoy play throughout their lives, often spontaneously pouncing on another in mock ambush, or chasing pack members around in a game of canine tag.

As the pups mature, their play is directed more closely towards hunting training by the pack elders. Predatory behaviour like stalking, chasing, herding, scent following, digging for prey, catching and killing are all contained in various games played within the safety of the pack. This may start with hunting small rodents near the vicinity of the den. Later, they will accompany the rest of the pack on a mock hunt to introduce their new found skills to a herding situation.

Here, older members teach the pups how to run down prey by driving a herd to isolate its females and their young, all the while orchestrating a situation where they can encourage the pups to chase these youngsters of the herd. The more practice they get, the better the hunters they will be, assuring the pack of its survival.

Childish Dreams may be True

When I was a child, my mother would try to encourage me to read storybooks but the only books I was interested in were animal stories. I loved animals so much that I suppose it was no wonder that I often had dreams about animals.

One dream I remember clearly was a recurring dream, often coming back in different forms. It was about cavepeople who would bring dogs and other animals back to their camp for food. The dogs had puppies that were kept in separate cages and, when the cavemen were out hunting, the children would sneak away from their mothers and feed the puppies and even sometimes play with them. From this, a bonding would naturally grow. Later, when the grown-ups wanted to kill the puppies for food, the children would complain and cry until they were allowed to keep them as pets.

I forgot about these dreams until a similar situation happened in my family when I was about thirteen years old. A few months prior to Christmas that year, my parents decided to buy a duck and fatten it up for Christmas dinner, so my mother bought two small ducklings from the local market. My two sisters, however, took over the care and feeding of these ducklings and gave them the names of 'Duckie' and 'Quackie', even dressing them up and playing with them. All was going well until Christmas arrived and my father went out to the shed to get his axe in preparation for Christmas dinner. My sisters cried and pleaded with my father to spare the birds that had now become their pets.

Consequently, we had roast beef for Christmas dinner that year— and Duckie and Quackie lived to an old age!

This true experience, plus my childhood dreams, has given me a very strong belief that a similar situation happened to the domestic dog's ancestor, the wolf. Wolf puppies brought back to the cave for food were played with by the children, and a strong friendship and bonding occurred, resulting in the puppies being spared and growing up with our cavepeople ancestors as pets. This, I feel, is how the first domestication of wolves originated.

Strong bonds and friendships occur when children and puppies get together. This may be how dogs were first domesticated.

Similarities between Wolves and Domestic Dogs

As we have seen with the description of the ways of the wolf, there are many actions in our dog's behaviour that can be compared to that of its ancestor. There are countless stories of the faithful dog refusing to leave its troubled owner, of dogs saving their owner's children from drowning when they have fallen into deep water, or alerting their owner to eminent danger. The famous 'Lassie' books are full of these types of stories, most of which illustrate the very real characteristic traits of courage, intelligence and loyalty that the domestic dog shares with its ancestor, the wolf.

Humans have long taken advantage of these traits, using dogs to help them in many ways. We have trained dogs to help police, deaf and blind people, customs officers, search and rescue teams, farmers, builders, as transport (sled dogs) in the snow, and even to improve the morale of hospital patients. They really are the ultimate helpers for humans.

Just as the wolf uses its acute senses to interpret what is happening in its environment, so too does the dog. You might think that you will be able to conceal the fact that you are getting ready for a walk by being especially quiet, or changing the order of some of the actions in your routine. However, your dog will always seem to know exactly what is happening and get excited about its upcoming adventure in spite of your efforts! This often gives us the feeling that our dog can read our minds, and who knows, with their enormous intuitive ability, also inherited from the wolf, perhaps that is exactly what they are doing.

Every single action you make is being carefully monitored by your dog in such detail that it is hard for us to imagine. It is this very ability that the wolf uses to coordinate the pack and its activities. To the domestic dog, its owner and any family members are its pack. Our dog is constantly making an effort to synchronise with us and what we are doing. When we have to leave the house our dogs get restless as we prepare our departure, on the chance that it will be going with us.

When it is dinnertime our dog wants to eat at exactly the same time as we do. It will probably be waiting in or as near the kitchen as it can get while the meal is prepared. At times when we are resting or watching television it is happy to rest or sleep at the same time, although the moment you get up it will be alert and ready for action.

The most important factor in the way a dog's mind thinks is in relation to its behaviour and interaction with us, and the fact that it regards its owner(s) as members of its pack. With this, automatically, goes the hierarchy or 'pecking order' of the pack animal culture and we must learn to be mindful of this at all times. The pecking order in our 'pack' can constantly change depending on how we treat our canine pet, and either you or your dog will be regarded as 'Top Dog'. This book makes an effort to explain in detail how you can claim that position of 'Top Dog' and keep it, improving the behaviour of your dog and the relationship you have with it.

The amazing tenacity and staying power displayed by wolves while hunting is evident in every dog's daily life. Most of you would have seen, at some time, this same persistence when you have tried to stop your dog behaving in a certain way, at which it continued to go on and on to a point when you thought the behaviour would never stop! This, of course, is simply nature in action. These traits have been passed down to your dog from its ancestors through the genes. For wolves to have survived for thousands of years with the enemies the world has placed on them, they have had to be persistent, with a spirit of never giving up. Like them, our dog's tenacity is incredible.

If you spend some time at the local park you may have seen the stalking tactics in breeds such as border collies, or pointers displaying exactly what they were named for. Most of us have seen or heard about the amazing ability of cattle dogs herding sheep or cattle. All of these behaviours are natural hunting instincts passed down from the wolf. After catching or finding their toy, a dog may shake it or throw it around. Of course, it is really trying to kill the poor defenceless toy, just as a wolf would kill a small mammal.

The wolves' prey-carrying behaviour.

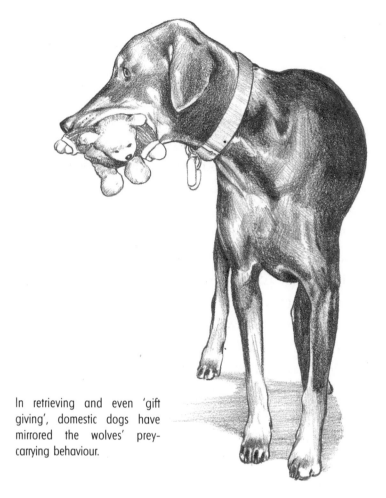

In retrieving and even 'gift giving', domestic dogs have mirrored the wolves' prey-carrying behaviour.

The instinct that urges wolves to bring food back to the den can also come out in our domestic dogs as retrieving and even 'gift giving'. Breeding has exaggerated this natural activity in golden retrievers and terriers. One Doberman I know will rush around looking for a ball or a piece of its bedding to carry when its owners arrive home, as if giving them a present on their return. It also uses this for attention-seeking behaviour at other times. Some dogs will pick their food out of their bowl and take it to another, more suitable place to eat.

The wolf's practice of burying surplus food in a cache near the vicinity of the den, or digging when prey has gone to ground, is also an instinct that carries across to domestic dogs, but in our homes the way this behaviour shows itself can seem rather confusing. Every dog lover knows of a dog burying a bone or other items in the backyard, but some of our four-legged friends bring this same behaviour inside. There are plenty of dogs that scratch at the carpet or a mat inside the house in an attempt to hide things under it. One of my clients has a dog that hides things under her bedding, using her nose to cover up the particular item with the hessian in her bed. Special 'keepsakes' have even been hidden behind cushions on the lounge chair. Behaviour that seems irrational to us has its origin in the natural behaviour of the wolf.

The instinctive action of a wolf pup licking its mother under the chin for regurgitated food can be seen when we return home from work or a day out. You would probably have noticed that your dog becomes so excited that it will jump up and try to lick you under the chin. This is a natural pre-wired reaction by our dogs, simply because they think that we have been out hunting and they are happy the pack has returned safely. Just like wolves, dogs are very social animals and prefer to be with their pack members at all times. A relatively unpleasant side to this is the translation of this instinct to our domestic dogs. In the wild, if the pups do not eat all of the food the mother has regurgitated for them she will eat it herself. Even though the regurgitating urge has probably been modified through breeding because we find it undesirable, this does explain the habit that most dogs have of eating their own vomit.

How often have you taken your dog for a walk and it has stopped at every tree? This behaviour with dominant dogs can go on and on until you start to wonder if it will ever run out of urine! If this sounds familiar and I'm sure for a lot of you it must, your dog is merely doing what has been naturally passed down from the wolf. Your dog is seeing itself as a high-ranking member of your pack and is marking its territory, letting the other dogs in your area know that this is its turf. High-ranking wolves spot trees with urine around the boundaries of their territory as a message to neighbouring wolves from other areas not to trespass! A wolf marking the territory will often scratch at the ground with its back legs after urinating or defecating. This is also thought to be territorial marking, with an effort being made to spread the scent across as wide an area as possible.

High-ranking wolves spot trees with urine around the boundaries of their territory, warning neighbouring wolves not to trespass.

The way that we treat our dogs can tend to keep their mental state like that of a puppy. In our efforts to keep domestic dogs manageable and obedient through breeding and training, we have created an animal that will be dependent on others for its whole life. We have adopted the maternal, care-giving role for our dogs with all the responsibility of housing, feeding and grooming them. Although adult wolves do retain their youthful curiosity and playfulness, juvenile characteristics displayed by some adult dogs, such as whining, jumping up, sticking to you like glue, etc., would never be seen in an adult wolf. This is care-seeking behaviour. Instead of being left back in the puppy stages, this behaviour can continue, being directed at the dog's owner through to the end of its life.

Yes, our domestic dogs have so many similarities with the wolf. The more we study and understand the way of the wolf, the more we are able to observe these similarities in our own dogs. Although we have hundreds of different breeds of dogs around the world today, some selectively bred over many hundreds of years to have certain traits, appearances and temperaments, they are all still heavily influenced by their forebears, the wolf. The factors that distinguish the different dog breeds are merely exaggerations of qualities inherent in the wolf.

The Ten Keys to Effective Training

KEY 1. Dog's Dinner

In the canine family, the leaders always eat first. This behaviour stems back to our dog's ancestor, the wolf. In a wolf pack situation, the leader of the pack, the alpha wolf, will take the underlings out hunting and will instruct them on how and when to attack their prey. However, once the quarry has been caught and killed, all but the alpha wolves (usually the most dominant male and female) will move away from the felled animal, allowing the leaders to eat first in respect of their high-ranking position. These 'superiors' eat the best parts of the animal and those lower down in the hierarchy eat increasingly slimmer pickings.

Humans have, through selective breeding, managed to change the way our dogs look from their ancestor but, we have only been able to change less than 15 per cent of their mind. Domestic dogs instinctively think and act as their wolf ancestors did in an enormous amount of things that they do. Especially when it comes to eating.

The relationship that we share with our dogs needs to be a canine-based relationship—one where the human always plays the Top Dog. To reinforce to your dog that you are the pack leader, you need to simulate the wolf behaviour mentioned above when feeding your dog in your home. Your dog must always eat after you. This is one of the main solutions to better behaviour from your dog and why it is the first key on the list.

dinner time

Your dog must always eat after you.

An adult dog should be fed once or twice a day, depending on your lifestyle and the condition of your dog. Your vet is the best person to discuss this with. However, if you are feeding your dog once a day, feeding it in the evening is probably the most practical. This is unless it is overweight, in which case, feeding it in the morning can help improve the weight situation, as it has all day to utilise its food intake.

Dinnertime

When feeding your dog, this is the procedure you need to follow. First, prepare your dog's food prior to you eating your own meal. Take your dog's dish to the spot where you would usually feed it but instead of placing the dish on the ground, place it in a high position, where your dog is unable to reach it. Leave it there while you go away and eat your own meal. After you have finished, go back to the place where you have left your dog's dish, have your dog sit (providing it will do this for you, and if not, this is something you can be working on) and after it sits, put the dish down and leave it to eat. Return after fifteen minutes.

If the food has been eaten, remove the plate, clean it and put it away. However, if food has been left, as it often is, pick up the dish and place it back up high (where you left it previously) and leave it there for a further hour. After this time, return and place the dish down once more and leave it again for fifteen minutes. If any food remains uneaten, remove the dish with the remaining food. If it is food that will spoil, throw it away. If not, save it for tomorrow.

Do not offer your dog any more food that day. Repeat this method for its next mealtime and each one after that.

So, let's look at what we have done:

a) we have prepared our dog's food and made it wait for it, as would happen in the wild. There, prey would be killed but pack members would have to wait their turn in the pecking order before they could eat; and

b) we have controlled the amount of time allowed at the food bowl, as in the wild they would get only one chance to eat their fill.

We have now successfully simulated the canine natural eating behaviour. This feeding procedure tells your dog that it is not the leader—you are. This pattern of thinking then flows through to general behaviour, improving your dog's understanding that you are in charge.

KEY 2. No Rough with Rover

Any form of aggression with your dog can promote a dog that may nip or even bite you, a member of your family, a friend or a neighbour. Children will often play competitive games with their dog that consists of pushing, shoving and tormenting. This behaviour should not be encouraged as it can promote aggression in dogs. Many severe dog bites happen in play and this quickly sends a message to the dog that biting of family members is accepted. Wolves normally do not show aggression towards other members of the pack unless there is a competition for dominance or another pack member steps out of its place in the hierarchy. In this case, both dogs will fight aggressively until one backs down. At that moment, the winner of the battle is proven to be the more dominant member over the losing wolf and is treated accordingly. Your dog actually sees rough play as a challenge for dominance. Once it reacts, and you or another member of your family backs down, it then sees itself as being dominant over that person. Consequently, it moves further up the hierarchy of your family.

Rough games promote aggressive behaviour and disrespect from your dog. If your dog does not respect you then it will perceive you as a weak creature. The dog will want, and have, its own way and will not do what you want it to. This is where bad behaviour sets in. In a dog's natural environment disrespect is not tolerated and higher ranking pack members will quickly put subordinates in their place.

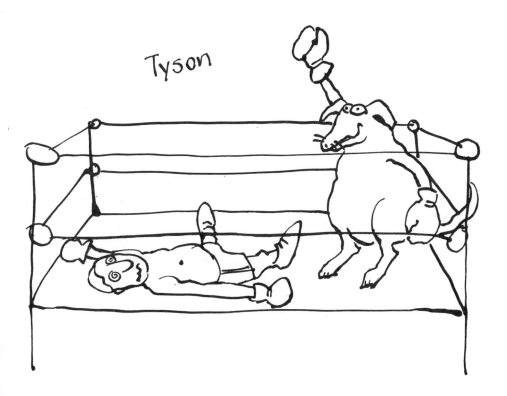

Tyson

Our dogs instinctively learn their life skills through play. Rough play leads to aggression.

Playtime is a natural and important activity for dogs and wolves alike. Wolves have often been observed at play, chasing each other around and bouncing out from behind a tree or rock to ambush another pack member in a playful way. Wolves learn their life skills from play and our dogs often do the same, instinctively. Yes, our dogs do need play, but because our dogs, like wolves, also use play to test one another's dominance, endurance, strength and fighting skills, our play needs to be non-aggressive and with us totally in control.

Dog Toys and Games

There needs to be two sets of dog toys—the ones you give your dog to play with and the ones you use to play with your dog. You, as the leader, need to be in control of the games.

So, let's say that you want to play 'throw the ball'. The first thing you need to remember is that the ball is kept away from your dog whenever you are not playing with it. This ball is the leader's ball. It is brought out by you, the leader. You throw the ball for your dog while it suits you, then when you have had enough, you stop the game, pick up the ball and put it away some place where your dog can't reach it.

While throwing the ball to your dog, if you find it won't bring the ball back and hangs on to it, then it is using this game as a dominance statement. It is saying to you, 'I'm in charge of this game—you will play by my rules'. If this occurs, you need to secure a light thin line to your dog's collar about three to four metres long. When you throw the ball and it doesn't want to bring it back, you simply reel your dog in like a fish and take the ball off it! Throw it again, repeating this procedure, until it realises that you are in control of the games that you play with it.

If you give your dog toys to play with, then these are its toys and should be played with only by it. Any special toys you intend using to play with your dog need to be kept aside until you are going to use them, then put away again once the game is over.

I find that games such as 'tug-of-war' only encourage your dog to challenge you. Chasing your dog is another way of letting your dog feel it is superior to you. If your dog runs off with an article you want and you chase it, your dog thinks it is smarter than you because you can't catch up to it!

By all means play with your dog regularly. It is a great activity. Apart from being fun for both of you, play helps you and your dog to bond even closer. Just be careful with the games that you choose. Your dog instinctively continues to learn about its relationship within your family hierarchy during these games. Like the wolves, you can use play as an important tool to reinforce your position as the leader of your 'pack'.

KEY 3. In the Den

The decision to have your dog sleep inside or outside is a personal one and either is fine, depending on your circumstances. However, certain rules apply to both situations.

If you decide to have your dog sleep outside, a kennel would be the best choice. This needs to be placed as close as possible to the back door because, as dogs are a pack animal, they want to be as close as they can to the other pack members, especially at bedtime. A kennel placed away from the house will nearly always be unused. Often a dog will sleep at the back door, even in rainy or wintery cold conditions, just to be closer to you, its pack member. Therefore, to give your dog every chance to use the kennel you have just bought it, place it by the back door. This gives your dog its own den close to where you are and makes for a happier, more relaxed dog. One that will, in turn, be better behaved.

Make the dog bed as bare as possible. We are often tempted to place an old blanket or old clothes in our dog's bed and this, I find, can sometimes cause behavioural problems. Clients of mine, that have had problems with their dog pulling washing off the line, have nearly always given their dog a blanket or some kind of fabric in their kennel to sleep on. In this case, the dog seems to think that any fabric whatsoever in the backyard is for its use. It then goes about pulling the clothes off the line to rest on and then proceeds to chew them up, much to the horror of its owner! In the wild, a wolf or wild dog would naturally keep its den clean, removing any rubbish, leaves or such that may have been blown into it. With some domesticated dogs this natural instinct is strong. That is why you will find that some dogs will remove the blanket or cloth that you have put in their kennel to keep them warm and comfortable. They will often pull it out and chew it up into little pieces as if to say, 'There you are—now try and put that back!' If you do want to place something in your dog's bed for comfort, I suggest you use a hessian bag. I have found, for some reason or other, dogs seem to accept this material better than anything else. People who use hessian bags in their dog's kennel seem to have less problems with washing being torn off the line than the owners who supply blankets or old clothes for their dog's bedding.

If you decide to have your dog sleep inside the house, the first rule for success is to make sure your dog is properly house trained, which I will cover in chapter six.

The place your dog sleeps within the house is crucial. Some people, for either security or closeness and bonding, will often allow their dog to sleep in their bedroom, or worse still, in their bed. Both of these arrangements, however, are totally unsuitable. In the wild, the leaders of the pack sleep in the best position and sleep together. The higher a wolf pack member is in the pecking order, the closer they sleep to the leaders, the male and female alpha wolves. By allowing our dog to share our bedroom, or our bed, we are sending a sound message to it that we see it as an equal. Unfortunately, there is no such thing as equality in the natural thinking of a dog and it will soon adopt a higher

Only the leaders of the pack sleep in the best position.

ranking position. If your dog is in any way even slightly dominant, this practice will eventually have it seeing itself as the pack leader and, in taking that role, will make its own decisions. The result is a dog that is very difficult to handle.

As much as we love our dogs, they must not be allowed to enjoy high advantages around our home. Comfort that we provide for ourselves in our environment, such as soft lounges, beds and cushions, are not necessary in a dog's world. Their domain is the floor and the ground. Giving your dog permission to use your creature comforts will inadvertently encourage it to be dominant over you.

A laundry or spare room away from your bedroom is normally a suitable sleeping place for your dog inside the home.

KEY 4. High and Mighty

Height is an extremely significant factor in the way dogs relate to each other. Often a dog will show its dominance over others by displaying certain body language that accentuates its height, no matter how tall or short that dog may be. Dogs often display dominance by carrying their tails high in the air with their ears erect (where their anatomy allows it) and standing tall, making themselves as high as they can. The leader of a pack of wild dogs or wolves will often climb to a higher vantage point to sit and observe its domain and the underlings in its pack. Lions often do the same, as this is part of the natural pack leadership instinct.

Our dogs, especially the more dominant ones, will use anything in the home to gain extra height. The higher a dog sees its rank in the pack, the more it will climb up on the furniture or anything else it can

In the wild, the leader of the wolf pack will climb to a higher vantage point to observe its domain.

The higher your dog sees its rank in your family, the more it will climb up on the furniture or anything else it can reach.

reach. That, of course, means lounges, chairs, tables, beds, high steps and often the outdoor garden table. So, keeping your dog off articles with height, either inside or outside the house, is important to having a well-behaved dog. Your dog's behaviour will definitely improve if you keep it at ground level.

I am often asked by clients who have small cuddly dogs if it is alright for them to have their dog on their lap whilst watching television. I tell these people that on the surface of things this may seem like an innocent, loving and caring activity to enjoy with their best friend. However, having your dog on your lap at any time, for whatever reason, is simply giving it a clear message, in its understanding of things, that it is your equal. As there is no equal in a pack structure, it will assume the highest ranking position as the leader (alpha dog), doing what it wants, when it wants to do it. This is an entirely natural response from a dog that sees its owner as a weak leader.

My suggestion, if you want your best friend to be well behaved, is to bring it next to you when watching TV, or when you are seated to have it on the floor. Your dog will soon get used to being there and once it accepts this, you will both be better off. You will have nature working for you rather than against you.

If you have trouble with your dog getting on furniture, simply put a lead on it when you allow it in the house and let it walk around with the lead trailing behind it. As soon as it gets on the furniture, simply take hold of the lead and pull your dog off by using a slow gentle pull—the key word being gentle. At the same time say in a firm manner, 'Aah aah'. Repeat this whenever it tries climbing up again and very soon your dog will respect the fact that the furniture is off limits to it and this bad behaviour will stop. By doing this calmly and quietly, in a matter-of-fact way without aggression, your dog will quickly learn. The way its mind works will have it seeing you as the superior, which is exactly what you should be.

accentuating height

Our dogs, especially the more dominant ones, will use anything in the home to gain extra height.

As soon as I can persuade a client to take this non-threatening approach with their dog and instead work with the dog's nature, the quicker the dog will do exactly what the owner wants and enjoy doing it.

KEY 5. Just Whisper

While visiting clients' homes where I have been asked to assist with dog behavioural problems, I have noticed that most of these people will shout at their dog to try to get it to obey them. The owners will often forcefully tell their dog to sit and when the dog does not obey, they raise their voice. If the dog still does not do what they want, they start shouting. This of course does not help. It reminds me of the story of an immigrant lady going through the check-out of the local supermarket in her new country. The young girl behind the counter asks her for forty-five dollars for her groceries. The lady indicates that she does not understand the cashier, at which the girl raises her voice. When the poor woman still does not understand, the girl almost shouts at her for the forty-five dollars. A gentleman standing in line steps forward to explain to the cashier that the woman is not deaf, she merely does not understand their language. This is exactly the situation we are in when we shout at our dog— we totally confuse it. The dog knows that you are angry but it does not have the slightest idea of why you are angry. There is no need to shout at your dog, it does not have a hearing problem, you just haven't taught it correctly.

Dogs hear our utterances in two distinct parts: they hear the tone of our voice and the sound it makes. If you were to say to your dog

You only need to whisper—your dog does not have a hearing problem.

'Good boy' in a loud, angry voice, your dog would think you were angry with it. On the other hand, if you say 'I hate you' in a low, soft voice, your dog will probably wag its tail and think you are being friendly to it. The loudness or softness of our speech when communicating to our dog is very important. If you want your dog to receive the correct message, you should never shout. Avoid confusing your dog.

I find one of the main causes for people raising their voice or shouting when trying to communicate with their dog, is when the dog does not obey a command. The owner thinks that by being forceful, the dog will comply with what they want. Often the reason the dog does not obey, however, is that a sentence is used for a command rather than a word, for example, 'Rover, sit down'. As dogs hear what we say by sound and not words, there are too many sounds in this sentence-command for the dog to clearly decipher the exact message. This is why one syllable word commands are important, and a better command for it, in this case, would simply be 'Sit'.

Another mistake that people often make is to keep changing the command word. This seems to happen especially in a family situation where each member of the family may use a different word for the same command. One family member may say, 'Come here Fido' (here we have four sounds), another may simply say, 'Come!'

With just these two examples it is easy to see how giving mixed messages through our inconsistency could result in a neurotic dog. I have often called on clients whose dogs have enormous behavioural problems and this practice of changing command words has confused the dog so much that it has been the main cause of the dog developing displacement activities, such as digging up the garden, and chewing the house down. By having the family use one-syllable words only and the same word for each command, the behavioural problems diminish rapidly.

In some cases it's that simple. People don't realise that a large amount of bad behaviour from their dog can be attributed to doing something as innocent as changing command words, which is something that most people do.

The reason we change command words, I feel, is that we somehow see our dogs as being like little children. In most cases a child of even a few years would normally understand the meaning, even if we change the word slightly. However, not so with our dog, as dogs hear by sound and not by pronunciation. You need to be saying the same words consistently, in the same way, otherwise your dog will be confused and won't respond to your commands. This is where we often become agitated and start raising our voice. The dog becomes confused and with confusion comes stress, hence, the bad behavioural problems brought on by stress.

Where we train our dog also has a consequence on the result of using certain commands. People often say to me that their dog understands the word 'Sit', but often will not do it. The dog will obey the owner in the backyard but not any other place. These people don't realise that dogs don't generalise. If you teach your dog to sit in the backyard it may not work in the street because being in a different environment changes the way the dog perceives things. So instead of shouting at your dog because it sat in the yard and will not sit outside, simply retrain it in its new environment. Then you only need whisper to have it sit for you.

Communication in wild dogs and wolves is virtually silent when these dogs are in close range of each other. Here they mainly rely on body language, such as a series of facial gestures together with movements of their ears and tail, combined with their overall posture. When reprimanding a subordinate a wolf will growl. Loud noises like howling are only needed for long-range communication.

To simulate the way of the wolf remember, don't shout, just whisper. By whispering commands and then raising your voice slightly when reprimanding your dog, your dog quickly learns when it is doing something wrong. As explained in chapter three, use dog language to voice your disapproval when your dog misbehaves, with an 'Aah aah!' It is a human sound that dogs relate to as a growl. This, you will find works magically—your dog will understand your commands because it will have to listen more carefully.

Try this technique and be patient with your dog—you will see a huge improvement in its behaviour.

KEY 6. Whisper Walking

Six out of every ten clients that call me about their dog's behavioural problems tell me they view walking the dog as one of the most unpleasant things they can do. Their dog pulls them down the road almost wrenching their arm out of its socket. An enormous amount of people I speak to on a daily basis have sustained injuries from simply walking the dog. So, let's look at the total walking situation and endeavour to alleviate this behavioural problem—a problem that ruins an experience that should not only be extremely pleasant for you and your dog, but also be healthy for both of you.

Let's start with the scenario that happens in most cases where your dog is in the backyard and you have decided to take it for a walk. What usually occurs is that you find your dog lead, go to the yard and when the dog sees the lead it goes ballistic. It jumps all over you and then you have a fight with it to actually get the lead on. You try and try as your stress level is rising, commanding it to sit over and over again until eventually the lead is clipped on! Away you go with a hyped up dog that has already shown you, even before you get out of the gate, that it is in charge of the situation.

Off to a Good Start

It can actually be very easy to put that lead on providing you do not get involved with all that pushing, shoving and shouting commands at your dog to behave. Simply set your mind before you go out to the backyard that you are not going to take your dog for a walk today until your dog sits calmly while you put its lead on. Now with this attitude, go outside holding your lead by the clip and say nothing. As your dog approaches you simply say 'Sit', in a low, calm voice, and only when your dog obeys your command do you bend down to fasten the lead. Usually what happens next is that your dog will jump up and start to be boisterous again. Stop and begin the exercise all over again but this time make sure you are standing as tall as you can in an upright position and don't move, even if your dog is jumping up. Say nothing until your dog settles and begin the same steps until you can calmly fasten the lead. Very soon you will find that your dog will sit quietly waiting for you to do so.

We greatly underestimate the intelligence of our canine friends. A dog with this behaviour sees an episode like this as a game. It gets itself so excited and worked up and is then rewarded for all its antics with exactly what it wanted, a walk. Why should it change its behaviour when it gets such successful results?

In life I have found that there are usually methods that sound good in theory and others that actually work. So, here I am going to give you a technique that may contradict some established training principles but works incredibly well if done correctly.

This special walking training technique requires you to walk at an extremely slow pace, a snail's pace in fact. Unlike fast walking which

I find excites the dog that pulls, and increases its adrenalin, the method I have developed quietly relaxes the animal, much like the slow pace of yoga.

After following the previous steps you will have succeeded in putting your dog's lead on in an orderly manner and are now out the front and about to start on your journey.

Whisper walking requires you to walk at an extremely slow pace—a snail's pace in fact.

Taking Control

Allow two pit stops for your dog to relieve itself, once you leave the front gate, while keeping it under control in a heel position. It is preferable that these tree stops are made away from your front lawn. Then try to refrain from allowing it any more stops along the way as these are just territory markers and you want it to concentrate on walking on your terms only.

With this out of the way, place the dog on your left side and make it sit. Your dog's front paws should be in line with your feet and its shoulder in line with your left leg. The lead should come across from left to right in front of your body and held in your right hand while anchoring it with your left in the control position. Keep your left hand approximately 6 to 7 cm away from the clip (for larger dogs) as seen in the opposite diagram. Hold your dog close to your left leg, short on the lead and walk as slowly as possible. Whatever you think walking slowly is, walk slower. Do not let your dog get in front of you at any time.

This exercise should be done on a concrete path or the equivalent to start with, to minimise distractions for your dog. Once it is under control and heeling correctly by your side without pulling, then, and only then, do I recommend you advance to a grassy area. If your dog tries to pull off to the right or left while walking along the path say in a firm and low, almost guttural tone, 'Aah aah'. If your dog loses traction, which will happen with bad pullers from time to time, simply stop, pull it back in line with you, count four seconds and then continue.

You should keep this procedure up for three or four days every time you walk your dog. With each outing, you will find it relaxes a little bit more. Then we move to the next stage.

When walking your dog, have the lead across your body from left to right, held in your right hand and anchored with your left. Keep your dog close to your left leg, short on the lead, and walk as slowly as possible. Do not let your dog get in front of you.

Start out the same as usual with your dog walking by your left side but now let go of the lead with your left hand and drop your right hand down so your dog is walking on a loose lead. It will probably surge ahead with its new found freedom. So, when this happens, take hold of the lead again with your left hand and pull the dog by your side saying 'Aah aah!' Then, as soon as it is by your side, let your left hand go and praise your dog. This only needs to be a simple, one stroke pat on the top of his head with a simultaneous, 'Good dog'.

When your dog has been conditioned to walk by your side, even though you held it there at first, you will be able to walk calmly down the street with a loose lead. When you need to stop, your dog will stand staying by your side. Again, if it moves away at first pull it back with an, 'Aah aah'. Praise the dog when it stays near you. Very soon you will have the best walking dog in the street.

KEY 7. How Dogs Learn

Dogs learn very quickly to avoid things and situations which are distasteful to them. They also learn extremely fast that a certain action leads to a particular event, either pleasant or unpleasant. For example, if you always go to the same cupboard to get your dog's food it will soon associate this action with it receiving its dinner. If your dog is food orientated, and most dogs are, it will get excited when you simply open the cupboard door. This is what we call 'classic conditioning'. Even if you are going to the cupboard for something completely different, your dog will show its excitement in anticipation of something pleasant.

This situation is the same as when you reach for your dog's lead and your dog associates the lead with a walk. It becomes excited, jumping and running around. However, if you only put your dog's lead on when it is bath time and it hates the water, chances are, your dog will run away to avoid you. Here the dog associates its lead with something that is unpleasant to it.

Both of these situations show how different events that happen in our daily lives make an imprint on your dog's mind, whether it is positive or negative. The secret to a dog learning, I find, is the W.I.I.F.M. principle, or, What's In It For Me.

Dogs, like many other creatures, look at what is best for them in any given situation. When I ask a dog owner who has a dog that won't sit when asked, if they have a problem with that dog sitting when offered its food, the answer is always the same, 'No, it always sits for its food'. It's amazing how quickly a dog will learn when it wants to. So, that is the key. Your dog will learn very quickly when it sees the situation is to its advantage. You simply need to place before your dog the opportunity to be rewarded and show it what it has to do to receive the reward, hence, reward training, which I will cover in chapter four.

Dogs also learn by association. You may get your dog's lead from its usual place and ask your dog to sit so you can put its lead on. The dog associates these familiar actions with going for a walk, so it gets excited as it links this with something pleasant that it likes to do.

Follow the Leader

Of all the creatures on Earth, I don't think there is a better observer than the dog. Watch your dog the next time you take it for a walk and take notice of its obsessive observation of anything and everything that moves: the cat in the distance; the car driving down the road; or that dog a street away, coming towards you. From the moment you leave home until your return, your dog will be constantly checking all of these things out—and more! So, is it any

Dogs are always learning throughout their lives and we, the carers, need to provide positive opportunities for them.

wonder that dogs learn from observing one another and their environment, which of course includes us?

Our dogs will also learn from experience. A dog barking at the back door which is eventually let in, will learn that constant barking has its rewards. The dog which comes up to the table when the family is eating and whines until someone gives it some food, will continue to beg for food in this manner because it has learnt, from experience, that if it displays this behaviour, it gets the food it wants—when it asks for it.

This is conditioning. It is impossible to sit a dog down like you would a child and explain something to it. Only through experience and association (conditioning) can your dog learn. Understanding this is what training your dog is all about. Dogs are always learning throughout their lives and we, the carers, need to provide positive opportunities for them to learn skills and good habits so that we can both live in harmony with one another.

KEY 8. Wear the Two Hats of Dog Management

To communicate more effectively with our dogs, I have found it a great advantage if we can change our way of thinking as we deal with them. It is as if we wear two different hats, one for human thinking and one for dog thinking. We need to be able to think in a canine way when interacting with our best friends. The simplest way I can explain this to my clients, when they are having dog behavioural problems, is to ask them to take their human hat off and put their dog hat on.

We need to be able to think in a canine way when interacting with our best friends.

We need to consciously realise that even though we may see our dog as part of the family, in no way is it a little fluffy human. As hard as it may seem to some people, your dog is a dog and it will always think like a dog. This is in no way meant to be demeaning—dogs are beautiful creatures—it's just that they need interaction and care suitable for a dog, not a human. This is where taking our human hat off and putting our dog hat on comes into play.

Having made this point, however, it is clear to see that dogs and humans do have many similarities and these traits are what endear them to us. They, like us, are very sociable animals. Like children, dogs love to play and are fun seeking. Wolves have often been observed in the wild playing chasing games and hide-and-seek with other members of their pack, purely for the fun of it. Dogs can also be jealous, like some humans. With these and so many other similarities, it is no wonder that we confuse dogs with ourselves, forever trying to communicate with them in a human way instead of a canine way. When it comes to a situation when our dog refuses to obey our instructions, we often get frustrated and impatient. This, in turn, confuses our dog and it becomes stressed, which promotes bad behaviour. To alleviate this problem we need to look at the situation from the dog's point of view, that is, put our canine thinking cap on and think like a dog.

So How Can We Think Like a Dog?

The more we understand about how wolves behave and interact with each other in their natural environment, the easier it is for us to see any canine problem from our dog's point of view. Its natural instincts will determine its behaviour. In this book I have given many examples of how wolves and dogs act in the wild. The more we use this knowledge to compare our home situations to what may happen in a pack situation, the closer we are to wearing our dog hat. We can manage our dog's bad behaviour better if we understand such things as the fact that dogs do not have malice in their nature. Clients often tell me of instances where they have come home late and their dog has pulled the washing off the line. The first thing they think is that they must punish their pet.

We need to realise that when we leave the house for work, or any reason, our dog does not understand these human activities. In its canine mind, it thinks it has been left behind while we are out hunting! It may pull the washing off the line as a security blanket as it waits for your return. Some dogs are insecure and stressed when left alone for long periods of time and use the clothes to lay on and comfort themselves. This is actually natural behaviour for an animal that is so socially oriented. The instinct of belonging to a pack is so strong that they do not like to be separated from the other pack members for any length of time.

Wolves will generally hunt together as a complete pack, working as a team to chase and bring down an animal, an animal that is often larger than them. The more of the pack that are 'on duty', the more efficient they are at making a swift kill. There are times, however, when some pack members are left behind, and this is usually when there are pups to be taken care of, or when a sick, injured or old wolf cannot take part in the hunt. In the case where pups are involved, at least the mother or baby-sitter wolf has the company of the charges they are looking after. Even so, the ones that are left behind when the hunt lasts for a long stretch of time can be very anxious by the time the pack returns.

What about the dog you have put outside because it has been naughty, and then it digs a hole in the garden? It is natural for you to think that this was done as a payback, when in fact this action is likely to be attention-seeking. Your dog is working at trying to get your attention and knows this will be effective. Even if you come out screaming at it, at least it has managed to get you out there. Having you with it, although you may be angry, is infinitely better than being outside alone. Dogs that do not have the correct type of interaction with people or their owners often crave attention, and any attention is better than none.

As for giving paybacks or harbouring malice—no, dogs don't think that way. Their thinking is more here and now. Your dog may avoid a previously unpleasant experience, like not coming to you because, just once, you were angry with it when it did. However, this does not mean your dog holds a grudge. This one bad experience it had has been imprinted on its mind.

If your dog sits at the back door and whines to be let in and you yell at it several times to stop but then eventually let it in, for your peace and quiet, it will always whine to be let in. It knows that it may take a lot of whining, and at first you may be angry, but eventually you will weaken. With this situation it learns that persistence pays. Here is another example showing why you must put on your canine hat, to understand that you are simply reinforcing this behaviour and letting your dog win. A dog that whines to get inside should never be let in until it sits there in silence. If it knows this is the only way it is let in, it will soon learn to stop whining and simply come to the door and patiently sit there.

Bad habits can easily be eliminated by simply understanding the way dogs think, and although we humans have traits such as malice and revenge to stimulate certain actions, dogs do things for entirely different reasons.

KEY 9. The Sense of the Canine

The brain of a human is complex and sophisticated with many more functions than that of a dog. However, a larger proportion of the dog's brain is used (compared with ours) for senses such as hearing and smell.

Listen Here

The dog's sense of hearing is far superior to that of humans. Their ability to hear is brilliant. Not only can a dog hear remarkably well but it can distinguish the most minute change in sound with acute accuracy.

The dog's hearing, like that of its ancestors, the wolf, is so sensitive that it can clearly detect high pitched sounds of up to 40 000 CPS (cycles per second) from kilometres away. The human ear can only detect sounds up to 20 000 CPS. This ability is useful while hunting in the wild where the wolf can hear the high pitched squeaks of small prey like mice. It is estimated that some aspects of a dog's hearing is approximately four times greater than ours, meaning that they can hear sounds from four times the distance we can.

I had a client tell me recently that her blue cattle dog, Bobbie, would always let her know when her husband was coming home by going to the front window and, with his muzzle, moving the curtains out of the way to look out. This was always done quite a few minutes before the husband actually arrived home. She calculated that her husband must have been streets away when Bobbie first sensed that he was coming home. To make this feat even more incredible, they lived on a busy road with dozens of cars driving by every minute. Bobbie never went to the window for any other car except that of his owner, apparently knowing the exact sound of his owner's car from kilometres away.

I am sure many of you would relate to this, as many of my clients have stories about similar incidents.

Dogs with Taste

Clients who have dogs that are fussy eaters often tell me that they change the type of dog food on a regular basis in an effort to stimulate their dog's appetite. However, they admit that this practice rarely works. This does not surprise me because dogs, unlike us, do not have large amounts of taste buds on their tongue. It has been noted in some research that dogs have less than one-third the taste buds that we have. I have found that dogs are mainly attracted to food by smell and texture. If the smell and texture of a certain food is desirable to a dog, that food will be eaten. The taste of the food is the least considered factor to a dog when it is offered food.

For wolves in the wild, living from hunt to hunt and scavenging in between, how much they eat is actually more important than what it tastes like.

Dogs will often eat their own faeces. No-one is quite sure what the reason is for this, but there are many notions, such as an inadequate diet or that it is attention-seeking behaviour. Nature also plays a part. A mother wolf, like our domestic dog which has puppies, will eat her puppies' droppings to keep the area clean. However, I feel the smell and texture of the droppings is also relevant as an influence in this sort of behaviour.

If this is happening with your pooch, the problem needs to be managed by picking up your dog's droppings immediately after your dog has been to the toilet. Also try sprinkling the faeces with a strong substance such as Tabasco sauce or pepper. This can be successful in eliminating the problem.

Some dogs will dig up an old rotten bone that smells revolting to us and chew on it as if it was a delicacy. As a child, I had a cross cattle dog which loved nothing better than to roll in my horse's manure, often eating some of it! He would then bound back to me in such a friendly, tail-wagging, show-off manner as if to say, 'Hey, look at me.

Aren't I beautiful?' Dogs on a trip to the beach have been known to roll about on the first dead fish or seagull they find on the sand, much to the disgust of their owner.

It is believed that this behaviour may relate back to the domesticated dog's ancestors. When wolves want to disguise their scent from the prey they are stalking, they often roll in that animal's faeces enabling them to get close enough, without detection, to catch their next meal.

Yes, our dog has strange taste habits, from a human point of view. However, the more we understand our dog's taste and food needs and the psychology behind their behaviour, the better equipped we are to train our dog and eliminate taste-related behaviour problems.

Wolves Smell the Roses Too

A dog's greatest asset would have to be its sense of smell. Throughout history, humans have utilised dogs' amazing sense of smell, from finding lost people caught in an avalanche or landslide to detecting illegal drugs while on police or customs duty. In Japan, dogs have been used extensively to find people after an earthquake. Here, as in many other similar rescue situations, sniffer dogs work relentlessly side by side with their human partners finding people buried by tonnes of rubble, showing once again the incredible sense of smell that they have.

Dogs have some 220 million receptors in their scenting machinery which gives them superior smelling ability, while humans only have around five million. They can smell and identify scent diluted to about one million to one and can manoeuvre their mobile nostrils around to help locate the source of the scent. Some breeds of dogs, like the bloodhound, even have parts of their nose shaped in such a way as to

A dog's greatest asset would have to be its sense of smell.

improve their sense of smell immensely, enabling them to do incredible feats such as tracking and finding lost people.

A dog's sense of smell has naturally evolved from its ancestors and, even though a wolf's smelling ability is outstanding, some breeds of dogs have been selectively bred over many years to enhance this attribute even further, resulting in a dog with an even greater sense of smell than that of the wolf.

I remember one incident when I was truly grateful for having a dog with a sharp sense of smell. It was in the mid-sixties and I had taken Duke, my first German shepherd, down to the local park after work for a spot of training. We had just finished the usual training routine—sit, stay, heel—which probably lasted for an hour altogether. Returning to my car, I realised that I must have lost my car keys somewhere in the long grass of this huge park whilst training Duke.

It was winter and although the time was only 5.30pm it was already starting to get dark. I tried to find the keys myself for about twenty minutes but by now it was getting hard to see in the failing light. In sheer desperation I thought, 'What do I have to lose? I'll try to get Duke to help me find my lost keys'.

I had only once given Duke some practice in what we call a seek back retrieving exercise whereby you teach your dog to retrieve an article with your scent on it. This exercise usually takes months to teach to your dog to the stage of competence, so after only one session of training I wasn't expecting a positive response. However, as I said before, I had nothing to lose.

So, I gave Duke the signal to seek the lost article by placing my hand over his nose to reinforce with him my sense of smell. I then gave him the command to seek, and sent him off. Away he went but by now it was very dark. As Duke's saddle was almost all black it was nearly impossible to see him now. Within about three or four minutes he came back without the keys, much to my disappointment. But I wasn't going to give up yet, as the alternative was a long walk home and no transport to work the following day! So, once again I gave Duke the seek back signal sending him off into the darkness.

I waited for what seemed an eternity but in actual fact it would only have been seven or eight minutes, when I saw Duke coming towards me with his tail wagging away and his eyes shining. Then I heard the sweetest sound, 'jingle jingle'. As amazing as it was, Duke had gone out in the dark and with the outstanding sense of smell that our dogs have, found a small bunch of keys in the long grass in a huge park and returned them to his human partner.

I was very emotional about Duke's incredible feat, especially considering the fact that he had received such little training in the exercise of finding lost articles. It is an event I will never forget. Yes, dogs have an incredible sense of smell that has been helping their human partners for thousands of years.

Through the Eyes of a Dog

In my daily work helping people who own dogs with behavioural problems, I often find that these people know little about how a dog actually sees things. Dogs simply don't see the world as we do and evolution has played a major part in this.

The main factor separating us from our dogs is the placement of our eyes in a frontal position. In early times, our cavepeople ancestors sat around campfires designing and making tools and weapons for the next day's hunt. Throughout the ages, the other activities that went to make up daily life, practised over thousands of years, significantly refined our hand/eye coordination and in turn, our binocular vision. As a result, our ability to focus on objects directly in front of us has increased.

Dogs, on the other hand, have poor binocular vision but excellent lateral (peripheral) vision to varying degrees, depending on the breed. The wolf is known to have very good lateral vision because of the placement of its eyes. Some breeds of dogs, because of selective breeding over many years, now have eyes which are positioned similar to that of humans. Although these dogs have slightly more vision to the front, it is still poor compared to ours and they depend more on the information they receive from their lateral vision.

Over the years my own dogs have mainly been German shepherds, and this breed of dog has the placement of their eyes more in keeping with the wolf. With this side placement of their eyes, their lateral vision is excellent. Although our dogs may not see as clearly as we do, frontally, their eyesight at a distance is very acute, especially with moving objects.

Many dog lovers will have noticed that their dog does not seem to be able to see something directly in front of its nose. One of my clients thought her dog's eyesight was quite poor, as it often had trouble seeing a toy or ball right in front of its face. But that very dog had no trouble barking at the slightest movement it noticed, through the front window, outside on the street!

A dog's ability to see colour is something I am regularly asked about. Even though dogs do not see colour as vividly as we do, it is believed that they do see in tones of grey.

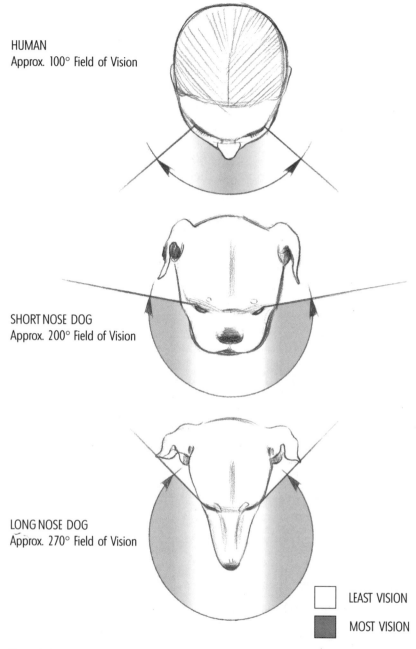

HUMAN
Approx. 100° Field of Vision

SHORT NOSE DOG
Approx. 200° Field of Vision

LONG NOSE DOG
Approx. 270° Field of Vision

LEAST VISION

MOST VISION

Dogs have poor binocular vision but excellent lateral (peripheral) vision to varying degrees, depending on the breed.

The eyesight of a dog is naturally designed for hunting. Evolution has helped advance the dog's hunting ability so much that the slightest movement of the smallest creature at a great distance out in the wild, can be seen by our dogs. This is why in obedience trials you will see competitors recalling their dog from a distance, throwing their arms up in the air to attract their dog's attention. The distance vision of a cattle dog is so acute that it can see the signal of the drover from a kilometre away. Our ability to get our dog's attention is greatly improved by our movement. Even the slightest hand movement will help you to attract your dog's attention, even at a great distance.

Yes, the more we understand the way our dog sees its world, the easier it is for us to learn how to better communicate with our best friend.

KEY 10. Dog's Native Tongue

Dogs communicate with each other using scent, body and facial postures and, lastly, voice. Unfortunately for us, our noses are inferior to the incredible ability of a dog's nose and as such, we have no hope at all of understanding the language of scent. We must rely on their visual form of communication, which is an exact series of movements and gestures we call body language. Dogs display their emotional state with the position of their ears, face, tail, hair, posture and body position. You may have noticed many subtle changes of expression in their face alone. Dominance is communicated through eye contact and this is why dogs observe us by watching our eyes.

Most humans either do not understand, or misunderstand this nonverbal language, which can make us and our dogs become very

Marcel
Dogue de
Marceau

Dogs talk in many ways and with many parts of their bodies.

frustrated. This is one of the main reasons that many of our dogs are stressed and why they totally ignore our attempts to communicate with them. They may have been continuously talking to us in their own way but because it is not a verbal language that we understand, we unintentionally ignore them, so in return, they ignore us.

Many a time I have heard a client say, 'My main problem with my dog is that it simply won't listen to anything I say'. To improve this situation, we need to start watching our dog's body language more closely and learn to understand the ongoing messages it is sending us. Dogs talk in many ways and with many parts of their bodies. If a dog wags its tail, we believe this is a friendly gesture meaning it is happy and friendly. Not quite so. People have often been bitten because they were lured into a false sense of security when a strange dog approached them wagging its tail. Aggressive dogs will often signal the fact that they are aroused aggressively by wagging their tail—but the wag is different to one that is friendly. The tail will usually move from side to side in a stiffer manner. The dog's ears will be pricked up and the overall posture of the dog will show it to be standing as tall as possible. All body language can be easily misunderstood if not observed carefully.

When a dog paws or jumps up at you, this can often mean the statement, 'I am in charge, I am the Top Dog'. Although, this can also be the action of an anxious, confused or submissive dog trying desperately to communicate. Inconsistent or harsh handling can encourage this sort of behaviour. If jumping up is used as a dominant display, a leadership program (incorporating The Ten Keys to Effective Training), along with motivational training, will help. If the problem stems from confusion, more positive and consistent interaction with the dog is needed to improve the situation.

Another gesture that is often misunderstood is the dog yawn. Dogs can yawn for a number of reasons—if they are sleepy; just after sleep through hyperventilation; if they are fearful; or to bring their stress levels down. Dogs will also often yawn if they are finding training difficult, in an effort to calm themselves, in the same way that you and I may take a deep breath to settle ourselves.

A gesture that is often misinterpreted is the dog yawn.

Greeting

All dog lovers have seen how a dog greets either its owner or another dog by wagging its tail, pulling its lips back in a grin or licking the face of the welcome 'friend'. Often a dog will bow. The dog will bounce their front quarters down on the ground, with their front legs outstretched in front of them. Their back legs are ready to spring into action at any moment. This is a common gesture that dogs use to invite another dog to play. If you have the time to visit your local 'dogs allowed off-leash' park, you will see body language in action, as there can be many dogs running around at these facilities, talking to one another. Here you have the opportunity to see the play bow as a greeting. A dog will often keep up this gesture until another dog takes up the offer to play.

Dogs often greet one another by wagging their tail, pulling their lips back in a grin or licking the face of a welcome 'friend'.

The licking of the face is an intriguing gesture, coming directly from the instinct of the wolf. When the mother wolf has returned from the hunt, her pups will lick her face to stimulate the mother to regurgitate food for them. In this way, they are weaned from milk to solids. Little do most dog owners know that when their dog gives them a 'kiss' on their return home, it is actually asking them to regurgitate some food!

There can, however, be varying meanings with most of the gestures that dogs use—as with our own body language. They must be seen in context with the circumstances and surrounding details taken into consideration. As an example, dogs also bow when they are about to attack wild prey, another dog or human. So be aware, there is more than one way to interpret a dog's gestures.

Aggression

It is not hard to recognise when a dog is showing obvious signs of aggression. The dog stands as tall as it can, with its hackles and tail up, snarling with its teeth exposed. What is not usually noticed, is the gradual steps its body has taken to get to this point. When the emotion of a dog changes, it can usually be seen in body language as flowing from one stage to another. From being calm, where the ears, tail and posture are relaxed, it moves to being alert—the tail and ears both prick up as the eyes open wide, peeled for any sign movement. If feeling threatened the emotion moves to aggression— the hair on the back goes up, the tail and hind quarters go up and the lips pull back. As the aggression increases the teeth are shown with a growling snarl. A dog showing this body language would bite if not approached the right way.

It's not hard to recognise when a dog is showing obvious signs of aggression.

Dominance

Dominance in a dog can be displayed without the use of aggression. If a dog is dominant it will be evident in every interaction and virtually everything that it does. Here are some things to look for:

a) it will always hold the longest eye contact;

b) its carriage will be tall;

c) it prefers to be up high (often on your furniture);

d) it will spread its scent as far and wide as possible (a female will even cock her leg while urinating); or

e) the dog will jump up at you.

Often a dog will use body slams or barging to dominate another dog, person or its owner, even the subtle action of standing on your foot is a display of dominance.

A wolf's dramatic display of dominance.

Submission

A dog will show submission by lowering itself in comparison to the more dominant pack member. This includes—ears down, hind quarters down and tail down, often between their legs. The head will be held lower than that of the challenger, with lips held in an horizontal position and sometimes curled up into what looks, to us, like a smile. To totally submit, a dog will lie flat on its back with its paws up and tummy totally exposed. This is the most vulnerable position for a dog.

I have a friend who has an adorable cocker spaniel called Charlie, which used this posture to his utmost advantage. Every time my friend tried to put Charlie outside at bedtime, Charlie would roll over onto his back. The family thought that this was cute even though it was

A dog shows submission by lowering itself to the more dominant pack member.

impossible to get Charlie out for the night. So, Charlie was left where he was. With a little help from myself, the family now realises that Charlie was passively being dominant over them.

In these circumstances, this submissive act was being used to control the situation. This is something our clever dogs often do.

Fear

Fear is a very real emotion for dogs and is often misinterpreted when mixed with aggression. The ears flatten back and the tail goes down between the legs (the fear biter position). They may crouch down with their tail between their legs if they become very anxious of the situation. It is easy to be bitten when fear is present if you do not interact with the dog correctly. Most dog bites to children occur when the fear biter position is assumed, as the dog is ready to bite even if the teeth are not showing.

If a dog is fearful of you (displaying fearful body language), NEVER pat it or even acknowledge that it is there. Don't look at the dog directly, as it perceives this to be a challenging gesture. Ignore it. On many occasions, if this type of dog is left alone, it will eventually come up to you and look for your attention and this is the best way to interact with a fearful dog.

We all have a tendency to underestimate our dog's intelligence simply because dogs are not the verbal communicators that we are. We need to be aware that most of our communication is verbal and most of our dog's communication is nonverbal. Their silent method of communication through body language is just as effective as ours. We just have to take the time and the effort to understand it. Use your eyes to listen to your dog from now on and see a beautiful new world of understanding and greater harmony come your way for both of you.

In Harmony with your Dog

As I think back to my second dog, Duke, this is how I feel he would have looked at life in our home and how his values and habits differed from ours.

Duke was purchased from a breeder at eight weeks of age, a German shepherd puppy that looked like a ball of fluff. I was then in my teens. When I first brought Duke home, I don't think he knew what life was about and his reaction to his new environment was that of confusion and fear of the unknown.

He whined most of the night, which was probably because he missed his mother and his litter mates and because of his new and strange environment. With care and nurture, he soon settled down and very quickly assumed he was one of the family (pack). At this stage of his life, all he wanted to do was play and sleep and I feel he just saw my sisters and myself as other puppies who were simply playmates. I remember him not taking too much notice of what we wanted him to do. It was obvious to us, by his behaviour, that he wanted to simulate our actions in every way. If we sat on the lounge, he wanted to sit on the lounge. If we ate at the table, he wanted to eat at the table. If we slept in a particular room, he wanted to sleep in that room. Because he was very sociable, our company was always important to him. Although young at the time, with limited experience, I nevertheless understood that canine management was important and my family did its best to limit Duke's access to only certain parts of our home. He was not allowed to get up on the furniture and beds as we realised that by letting him do whatever he wanted would be detrimental to his overall development.

As for values, I feel Duke's canine values were different to our human values in many ways. For example, what we saw as an expensive and valued table would probably have only been seen by him to be a large piece of wood on which, to the horror of my mother, he could exercise his jaws! On the other hand, toys always seemed to be very valuable assets to him.

As Duke grew older, he started listening more to what we said to him and seemed to show better understanding of what we wanted. I feel he started to see us as older animals and leaders and gave us the respect that dogs accord, in their natural world, to those higher up in the pecking order.

At this time in his life, I felt some formal training was in order. At first, Duke was confused as to what it was all about, but as dogs are creatures of habit, the more familiar he became with the training, the more confident and competent he became in responding to basic commands, even doing one or two tricks, which he excelled at and seemed to love. Dogs need a challenge and I felt Duke eventually looked at training as a challenge and enjoyed the stimulation it gave him.

These days, we often see the cutest dogs in television and movies that seem to understand everything that is said to them and are portrayed as having the same values and similar habits to ourselves. This often gives us the wrong impression that dogs are all but human. In the real world, dogs belong to a different species to humans and their thinking and values are different to ours in many ways.

Clients will often say to me, 'My dog thinks it's human', because of the way their particular dog acts. However, please remember your dog will never think of itself as human, rather—if anything, it sees you as another dog.

3

Putting the Keys into Practice

Boss's Last Chance

On walking up the garden path of a client's home recently, I couldn't help but wonder why people would wait so long to ask for help with a vicious dog. A dog that had already savagely bitten three members of their family.

To reach the front door I had to go through a two-metre wire gate with a sign on it reading, 'Beware of the dog'. Not wanting to go into an unknown situation with an angry dog on the premises, I shook the gate and sang out trying to attract someone's attention. A very anxious young lady in her early twenties greeted me and after assuring me that her dog was tied up, I was ushered into her home.

The whole family had gathered for this meeting, including her mother, father, grandmother and two brothers, both of whom had been bitten some time ago. Just recently her mother had been bitten viciously while trying to give the two-year-old cattle dog its food. All members of the family were terrified of this dog, although they loved it dearly, and they gave me the story that had led up to this point.

After the most recent biting incident, the father had taken the dog, named Boss (a fitting name indeed), to the local RSPCA to be put down. As he was making the sad journey home his daughter called him on his mobile telephone. She was in tears pleading with her father not to have the beloved animal put down. The young woman assured her father she would get professional help if he would just give Boss one more chance. The father explained that it was too late and that he was already on his way home without the dog. This loving father did not need too much more convincing to turn his car around and hurry back to the RSPCA with the hope that, indeed, it was not too late.

On arriving, the staff at the counter told him that Boss had probably already been euthanased but they took him down to the kennel to check all the same. The veterinary assistant informed him that the dog had been given its first injection to sedate him. The father asked if he could go into the cage and retrieve his dog. On hearing this, the staff were worried that he would be attacked by the ferocious animal and much discussion was had before they eventually gave him permission to enter. The man cautiously entered the cage to find Boss looking up at him in an aggressive manner. As he spoke to the dog there was an immediate change in Boss. He wagged his tail and licked his owner compulsively in an extremely friendly manner. This dog turned out to be one of the lucky ones. He was saved and taken back home that day. Most, of course, are not so fortunate.

That afternoon the daughter rang her local vet explaining the terrible situation and asked to be referred to someone who could help.

As it happened I had already been of service to one of their clients who owned a dog with similar behavioural problems.

Here was an intelligent family who, like so many of us, just did not understand the way a dog thinks. As a puppy, Boss had growled whenever anyone had tried to take a bone, or toy he was playing with, away from him. His owners thought it was so cute to see this little ball of fluff being so cheeky. As this pup grew into a dog, no-one ever touched his toys or food and if he growled at any of the family members they thought it best to simply leave him alone.

Boss quickly learned how to get his own way. He was inadvertently being trained that if he wanted his own way, or was not happy with the slightest thing the family did, he only had to growl and they would give in to him. This increased his aggressive behaviour, until he eventually saw himself as the supreme leader and this family as his underlings. They naturally had to be reprimanded more severely as his power and aggression increased. Boss' aggression also escalated as he grew older, as it does with many dominant dogs, because dogs reach full maturity in assertiveness and aggression between two and three years of age.

I will never forget my first encounter with Boss, which was in the owner's backyard. I had insisted that two collars and two leads, working independently, be placed on him before I risked life and limb to go out and analyse him.

The daughter and son of the family, both in their twenties, were holding him tightly and as I stepped down to the backyard from the safety of the house, I once again asked them to make sure that Boss was securely held. There were only four steps from the back door to the yard but by the time I had reached the bottom step, Boss was already frothing at the mouth. If he was free, he would certainly have savaged me. On assessing Boss, I knew I had a difficult assignment ahead but as I like a challenge, I was very confident that something could be done with this dog. He had become extremely aggressive and antisocial because his owners, like most of us, did not know how to rear and interact with a dominant dog.

Boss had a very bad case of Top Dog syndrome and, although he was genetically predisposed to aggression, a large portion of this dog's problem was learnt behaviour. Experience has also told me that in a dog's world, if it is not reprimanded for certain behaviour, in its eyes we are endorsing that behaviour. However, this does not apply to attention-seeking behaviour.

The family was put on a leadership program, whereby they had to be dominant with Boss but not aggressive in any way, continuing to be kind and caring. Dogs need consistency. If today we allow our dog to sit on our furniture, then if it doesn't suit us tomorrow and we don't allow this behaviour, we confuse our dog. This inconsistency can make a dominant dog aggressive.

This type of interaction was occurring with Boss on a regular basis, so I suggested that the inconsistencies stop. The whole family got behind fixing this serious problem and within weeks, with their cooperation, I was able to get Boss to act in a sociable way.

This vicious blue cattle dog's future had not been looking too bright. There was a huge chance that this creature would face the dreaded green needle, or worse still savage a child or a family member. Boss and I are now good pals and his biting of the family has completely stopped. He is truly a changed dog.

Although Boss is instinctively a dominant dog, the family now know how to manage the situation and that is what owning a dog is

Boss had a case of Top Dog aggression which was largely learnt behaviour.

about. Above all, be consistent, be dominant (not aggressive), be kind (not spoiling), manage the situation, and the time you put into your dog's management will have its own rewards.

Understanding Aggression

I consider aggression as the most serious behavioural problem still prevalent in domestic dogs today. This has been passed down genetically from the wolf.

A dog has three natural defence response modes:

1. fight
2. flight
3. freeze

Fight

A dominant-aggressive dog, if challenged in any way, will fight to the finish with all the ferocity it can muster. As some dogs have enormous power and with some breeds being especially developed for fighting other ferocious animals, they are very well-equipped for battle and can inflict enormous damage in a matter of seconds.

Flight

Fearful-aggressive dogs are the ones that people are mostly bitten by. This type of dog will often show fear and move away, going into flight mode. This can give us a false sense of security and cause us to take unnecessary risks that we may not otherwise take. A fearful dog can often attack with extreme ferociousness and inflict horrendous damage if it is prevented from going into flight mode by being caught or cornered. This type of dog can often feel that its very survival is being threatened by us and that it is actually fighting for its life.

Freeze

I have seen dogs charge at each other in such a way that you would think they were going to kill each other. However, as they come into contact with one another, they stiffen up and hardly move. They growl in a low tone at each other and move very, very slowly in a turning motion, but because neither starts to fight, or back down, they slowly part without a fight. A kind of dominance stalemate. A dog that freezes but shows no sign of fear will rarely be attacked.

I have found it extremely useful to understand as much as possible about the workings of a dog's mind, their rituals and why some dogs have aggressive tendencies. One of the most common aggression problems I encounter is what I call 'Top Dog aggression'.

Top Dog aggression usually comes about when a dog wants to dominate us. Dogs in their natural environment don't expect equality, their minds don't work that way. There is no democracy in a dog's world. Top Dog aggression usually occurs in male dogs between two and three years of age and, in my observations, this aggression is often directed at members of the dog's family, who the dog sees as its pack members. Often the slightest action can provoke Top Dog aggression, such as trying to put the dog out at night or taking a bone away from him. One client of mine had a dog that liked to sleep under the table, and any time she tried to put him outside, he would growl and then nip if she persisted.

As I have said, Top Dog aggression is often inherited genetically, but our interactions with our dog can also bring out aggressive tendencies. If our dog sees us as a weak leader and he is dominant, then he may assume the leadership position and put us in place by growling or even biting us if we challenge his authority. A dog exhibiting Top Dog aggression may only need us to look directly at him, or speak loudly to him, to stimulate aggression in him. This

Calm, yet alert.

Unsure, yet submissive.

Ready for action, confident, dominant.

Non-confrontational, submissive, non-threatening.

More assertive, dominant, in control, aggressive.

Totally submissive, trying to get own way, or prelude to play.

Aggressive.

I am being threatened, I may bite, fear is present.

Back off, I may bite.

If your interaction is not right, I may nip you, some submission.

I'm not sure of the situation, but push me and I'll bite, less fear is present.

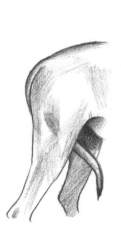

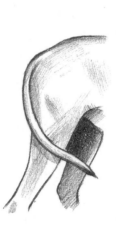

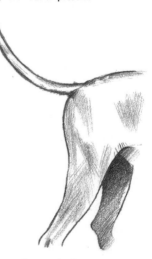

Very anxious, submissive, unsure of the situation, worried.

I don't like the situation, I'm worried, submissive.

I'm ready for action, either good or bad, I'm confident and dominant.

is because he feels we are challenging his hierarchy position. This type of aggression in a dog is mainly encountered by well-meaning, caring owners who, unfortunately, give in to their dog on a regular basis, letting it get its own way by treating him as an equal. As I mentioned previously, there can be no democracy in a human-dog relationship, it needs to be a dictatorship. A fair dictatorship, but with you as the dictator.

Helping Dad Dig the Garden

I recently called on clients, Bill and Sally, who had an eight-year-old black labrador-cross called Gypsy, that had taken to totally demolishing her owner's backyard by digging massive holes.

On arriving at the owner's home, I was informed that this dog had never dug a hole in its life up until now. After asking a few questions I found out the problem had only started about six months previously. Bill and Sally were a couple in their early thirties without children. They both could not find any reason why their dog started digging, as there had been no change to their lifestyle that they could think of. They still fed their dog in the same way, they interacted with the dog in the same way, so the only thing they could think was that the behaviour was being caused by something of a neurological nature. They thought Gypsy may have a physical problem which had brought on this behaviour, maybe due to her advancing years.

After about fifteen minutes, the owners took me out to their backyard to meet this mischievous dog. Gypsy sheepishly came up to me, smelt me, then moved back away from me. This is not a normal reaction from a dog of this age that has been properly socialised.

I asked for a lead to be put on Gypsy, so that I could walk her around the yard and observe her general behaviour. This poor dog had most of the hair missing from her lower back. The owners had been treating this problem for the last five months as an infection, thought to be brought on by flea bites.

As I walked Gypsy around the backyard, it was apparent to me that this dog was stressed. I could see that this labrador-cross had a very gentle nature and it was quite apparent that she had no previous obedience training. I gave her a couple of easy exercises, such as, 'sit' and 'stay' and, although these exercises were a new experience for her, she learnt very quickly.

After about twenty minutes, I went inside and sat back down at the kitchen table with the owners. I told them that Gypsy was an intelligent, sensitive dog but was very stressed. I added that I felt that this displacement activity of digging was being brought on by stress and anxiety caused by some change in their life, environment or some traumatic incident in the dog's life. They could not think of anything that might have caused the problem. By chance, Sally mentioned that the only thing that had changed in the family situation was that Bill had lost his job six months earlier. Then it all came out. Piece by piece the puzzle unravelled. The more Bill talked, the more the cause of the problem revealed itself.

When Bill had lost his job six months earlier, financial problems had caused the couple to start arguing—something that was rare up to that point. Bill was a smoker and when he and Sally had an argument, he would go out to the back steps and have a smoke. He admitted that often when that happened, Gypsy would come up to him for a pat and because he was anxious himself, he would shout at her to go away.

Gypsy did not understand this aggressive behaviour from her owner and as her anxiety increased she started digging to relieve the stress. On finding holes in his well-cared-for garden, Bill would scream at Gypsy, then start to smack her. This, of course, would stress Gypsy more and she would dig more holes. The angrier Bill became, the more holes Gypsy dug, a classic catch-22 situation. Both Bill and Gypsy were reacting to each other's behaviour, and this is often the cause of many behavioural problems.

I suggested to Bill that if he is feeling agitated he should sit at the front door in future and work on rebuilding his relationship with Gypsy. He should take her for walks, a practice he had stopped when she commenced digging because he thought it would teach her a lesson. (In fact it made the situation worse).

Two weeks after my visit, Bill rang to say that since he had started to rebuild his relationship with Gypsy, she had stopped digging and the hair on her back had started to grow. He told me he had learnt a valuable lesson out of this experience and that was that anger and shouting had no place in reprimanding dogs. Bill said that if he needed to reprimand Gypsy at any time he now simply said 'Aah aah' in a firm voice but without the shouting and without the anger.

Gypsy's case, once again, brought home to me the importance of not shouting at our dogs and never ever smacking them. A firm 'Aah aah' is all that is needed. Then, immediately, when your dog stops the behaviour you are discouraging, you simply say, 'Good dog'. If, like Bill, you follow this simple procedure, you will soon have a better behaved and happier dog that will soon be doing its best to please you.

Understanding Stress and Anxiety

Stress is a natural part of life, but there are times when we feel overloaded with the demands of the day and arrive home feeling uptight and irritable. It is the same with dogs. They too can suffer from stress, and some dogs are better at coping with stress than others. Dogs that are emotionally sensitive are more likely to be easily stressed. For instance, a dog that is unsure of its position in the pack can often become stressed because of this insecurity.

Statistics show that dogs that have been rehoused from animal shelters often get separation anxiety when left at home alone. Regardless of the reason they were surrendered, they probably feel they have been abandoned once again when their new owner leaves the house, and this fear stresses them greatly.

Stressors (the cause of stress) can include loud noises and other fears such as height, water, thunder, rain, strangers, unfamiliar objects and, as mentioned above, the fear of being left alone.

Sensitive dogs that have been smacked by their owners often become so stressed and anxious that they go into a freeze position. This is a state of helplessness where the dog feels it cannot escape its attacker so it literally freezes in motion.

The unknown can also make a dog anxious of being hurt or abused. Dogs can even wet themselves or defecate because of stress and fear. When stressed, dogs may carry out what is known as displacement activities such as excessive chewing, barking, howling, and scratching to escape (especially if shut in a room for a long period) or the excessive digging which Gypsy was doing. The way to relieve stress in our dog is to analyse the cause and alleviate it, as we did here with poor Gypsy.

Fear of the Unknown

Snoopy, a dainty, frail little whippet with a sensitive nature, had already been to four homes by the age of twelve months, when I was called in to give this frightened little dog some assistance.

Snoopy's new owners had rescued him from their local animal shelter and they realised very quickly why such an adorable little cutie had been to so many homes. The very first time Bill and Diane left Snoopy alone, the neighbours said that he had barked all day and that this behaviour continued every time the couple went out. It got to a stage, just before I arrived on the scene, where one day Diane left Snoopy to go to the shops for less than an hour and by the time she arrived home, Snoopy had chewed both of his front paws and blood was everywhere.

In sheer desperation, Diane went out the very next day and bought a large wire crate. Snoopy's erratic behaviour had prevented Diane from leaving the house, except when it was absolutely necessary. Two days after Diane had purchased the crate, one such situation occurred and Diane had to go out. Before leaving, she placed Snoopy in the large crate, giving him a toy to play with. She tried to comfort him by telling him that his mother would not be long, as we often do, somehow thinking our dog will understand us.

Diane was away for less than two hours and, on returning, was not prepared for what she found. Again there was blood everywhere. Snoopy's paws were covered in blood and it was all throughout the crate. Diane was devastated. She wiped Snoopy's paws and quickly took him to the local vet. Although there was no permanent damage, Snoopy had cut both front paws from clawing at the wire enclosure in a frenzy. Diane was totally distraught and this is when she decided that Snoopy had to go for his own sake.

Diane rang her local animal shelter, but on speaking to staff there, was told that if they once again accepted Snoopy and tried to rehouse him, it would not be fair to the next owner and that, in fact, it would only cause the problem to get worse. They encouraged Diane to give me a call.

Diane rang and spoke to me straight away. Although I was totally booked out for the next month, I rearranged my appointments so that I could tend to this serious matter immediately. I arranged for both Bill and Diane to be home when I called and as we sat around their dining room table, discussing the events that led up to this dreadful situation, it was apparent to me that this young couple had tried extremely hard to give Snoopy a good home and had been kind and caring to this little creature. Because he had been placed in so many homes, they were of the opinion that none of the other owners had given this dog enough love and attention and this was why Snoopy's adoption had not worked out with the others.

Bill told me that he would often sit in the evening after dinner and watch television with Snoopy on his lap. Bill said that Snoopy seemed to love this and he, understandably, thought that this caring gesture would help Snoopy accept his new family even more. However, my experiences have taught me that this is not so. After discussing with Bill and Diane their daily interactions with Snoopy, and spending considerable time with this little dog, my observation was that Snoopy was an intelligent, sensitive animal that had become fearful because of his concern about being discarded once more. Because of this fear, Snoopy was suffering from an extreme case of insecurity and separation anxiety.

I placed Snoopy on a strong emotional strength-building program, which included long walks and being outside more often. Also, sitting on Bill's lap while watching television was prohibited because this was contributing to the problem of over-bonding. This program was designed to make Snoopy more independent, which in turn would build up his inner strength.

Snoopy was on a meat-only diet and I suggested that a change would be helpful, so a complete dry food diet was slowly introduced. As we know, dogs, being carnivorous animals, need protein in the form of meat. However, I find that dogs with a balanced diet, including proteins, carbohydrates and vegetables, seem to be better able to handle stress.

Snoopy was also given something to chew on whenever Diane went out. She was asked to initially leave the home for only small periods of time, so Snoopy could build up his confidence that she would indeed return, then gradually extend the periods away over the next few weeks. During the next two weeks I rang Diane two or three times to check how Snoopy was going and made one more visit. After only four weeks, there was a noticeable change in Snoopy's self-confidence and Diane was able to leave Snoopy unattended without experiencing the previous devastating problems. Snoopy had settled down, his stress levels were much lower and he had become a happy, more confident dog. Diane now has peace of mind when she leaves Snoopy home alone and says that she and Bill are delighted that they are now able to share their lives with Snoopy.

Interacting with our dogs the wrong way can often make them totally dependent on humans and this can have devastating effects on our best friends. Our dogs need love, attention and kindness but a natural canine routine is vital to their wellbeing, otherwise they can become greatly affected emotionally, fearing to be left alone even for the shortest time because they fear we may never return and they will have to fend for themselves.

Love and care for your dog, however make sure you act in a consistent and responsible way so your dog does not become totally dependent on you and become an emotional cripple.

Understanding Fear

Recently I was commissioned by a client to travel to Melbourne to help with a fearful Rottweiler called Brodie. This dog's owner, Pam, a breeder with many years of show experience, had recently returned from a trip to Ireland, where she had purchased the six-month-old Rottweiler. On arriving in Australia, the poor dog was mistakenly taken to Sydney, instead of Melbourne, and was left in a crate in the sun for a time. When the crate was picked up it was accidentally dropped and Brodie had to be removed from the crate with a catching pole. After this traumatic ordeal, the dog went to another strange place in quarantine for a month. Whilst Brodie was at the quarantine centre, Pam would visit him regularly, however Brodie was now fearful of people and would run away from her, no matter what she did to entice him to her. After the month's quarantine was over, Brodie was taken home by Pam. By this time Brodie was devastated, jumping and twitching at the slightest sound or movement. Pam found it almost impossible to put a collar or lead on Brodie. No amount of coaxing or offering of a treat would get him to stay still enough to enable her to put a collar and lead on him.

With all these traumatic experiences, is it any wonder that this dog was fearful and stressed? These, and similar life experiences, are the ruination of many a dog. However, if you have this problem, don't despair, because this type of fear can be learnt from a perceived hostile environment and, therefore, can be changed with the right care, techniques and patience.

Avoidance is a natural canine reaction, and a fearful dog's 'avoidance triggers' are very acute. The slightest sound or movement from almost anyone towards a fearful dog could alarm it, with the dog invariably going into fight or flight mode, or at the very least displaying fearful body language such as tail between the legs, shying away from people and dropping to the ground.

Learned fear can even come from the dog's mother. A fearful bitch has a huge influence on her offspring and can pass her fear onto her vulnerable youngsters.

More people are bitten by dogs that are fear biters than for any other reason. If a dog is fearful of you (displaying fearful body language), NEVER pat it or even acknowledge that it is there. Don't look at the dog directly, as it perceives this to be a challenging gesture. Ignore it. On many occasions, if this type of dog is left alone, it will eventually come up to you and look for your attention and this is the best way to interact with a fearful dog.

Fear can also be genetic and could be passed down from the parents or ancestors in the genes. This is why it's a great advantage to meet a puppy's parents before choosing your dog. A dog with genetic fear can sometimes be helped but it can take a long time.

Fearful dogs need lots of socialising with other dogs and with people. They also need to be familiarised and desensitised with the everyday environment to accept noises such as vacuum cleaners, motor mowers, car noises, loud bangs and thunderstorms. The desensitising process needs to be done slowly at first, at low volume and at a distance. A tape recorder can be useful for this exercise as the volume and distance away from the sound source can be adjusted as required. After starting with low volume, gradually increase the volume of the sound, while staying at that same distance. When you have reached a stage where there is no reaction from the dog, decrease the volume once again, so as not to disturb it as you bring the dog closer to the sound source. Then, gradually increase the volume at this distance. At each stage decrease the volume initially, then gradually increase the volume, before moving closer still. If at any time the dog reacts badly to this stimulus, go back to a point where the dog did not react and start again. Then continue slowly.

A treat should be used in conjunction with the above exercise. When your dog does not react adversely to the stimulus of the noise, treat it. If your dog does react in a negative manner, then it does not receive a treat.

To deal with fear of any kind, we need lots of kindness, patience and to exercise consistency with our dog. When the right techniques are employed, in most cases, that fear will dissipate.

Dog Time Management

With the hectic lifestyle most of us lead in modern times, the skill of managing our time to include our dog's needs is most certainly necessary if we want to have the type of relationship that will give us a well-behaved and happy dog.

I recently called on clients, Brian and Lyn, who had behavioural problems with their eighteen-month-old standard poodle, Fifi. Brian and Lyn had a four-year-old daughter who went to kindergarten, while they were working at their own small business. The problems they were experiencing included Fifi jumping on them and their friends, chewing the back verandah, digging up the yard and barking continuously.

After taking an in-depth profile of the family and the dog, I perceived the behavioural problem to be caused mainly through boredom together with some separation anxiety. This family never walked this poor little dog, or played with it, never gave it toys to play with or even a bone to keep itself amused. In fact, the dog had very little interaction with the family.

On giving my opinion to Brian and Lyn on what I felt was needed to alleviate these problems, I was told by Brian, 'We don't have time to walk or play with our dog. The best we can do to enrich her life is to put some toys in the backyard'.

While I had been talking with Brian and Lyn in their home, I had noticed how caring and loving they both were with their daughter. In response to this observation, I said, 'Brian, no disrespect, but tell me, if you and Lyn were not here any more to look after your daughter, and that responsibility was passed to someone else, how would you feel if your little girl was neglected because those people said there wasn't sufficient time available?'

Brian looked at me harshly for a moment but said nothing. Then, after a while, he said, 'John, point taken. We love our daughter and I suppose if you care enough, you find time. What do you suggest we do?'

This family now gets up a little earlier in the morning to walk their dog and plays with it every other night when they arrive home. They also do some training with her and, consequently, their relationship with Fifi has improved immensely. Her behavioural problems have all but disappeared.

Why Some People Persevere

I feel there are many people in this world who, unfortunately, should not own a dog. I may be criticised for making this statement, however, I feel it must be said. My mother used to say, 'John, there are two things one can say—the truth or something that sounds good', and right or wrong, I prefer the truth.

I often meet people who simply don't have either the time to devote to caring for a dog or, alternatively, the right temperament to manage one. These people, in sheer frustration, often scream and shout at the animal and eventually even resort to smacking their dog if it won't do what they want it to do—not realising that the dog, more than likely, doesn't know what they want. Because of these problems they start ignoring their pet.

However, whatever the reason, be it lack of time and commitment or lack of understanding, a dog just doesn't understand why its owner behaves in this way. Without attention, guidance and caring interaction, the dog is invariably going to get bored, becoming even more out of control. Stress may also set in. Hence, we see all sorts of behavioural problems arising, such as gardens being demolished, furniture being chewed, endless nuisance barking, and even a dog becoming a biter. A large amount of these activities happen because of constant neglect.

On the other hand, I meet dog owners who give their dog nothing but caring and kindness yet still have lots of dog behavioural problems. I have seen some of these people in despair because they feel they have done everything possible for their dog and, by way of reward, it has almost wrecked their home and caused huge arguments with their partner. So, is it any wonder that many a desperate dog owner has seriously contemplated getting rid of their dog? Despite this, because these people can still remember bringing a little, helpless, furry creature into their home—nurturing and caring for it, as they would a child, they won't give it up no matter what. Some people persevere to a point where they have a dog that, unfortunately, virtually rules their whole lives.

I recently had an article published in a dog magazine (*Dog's Life*) about a business lady who worked from home and was attacked and almost bitten by her dog every time she attempted to answer the phone. She had tried everything she could think of to stop this behaviour until the only alternative, she thought, was for the dog to go. However, because she loved the dog so much, when it came to the crunch she persevered, even though her little dog certainly made her life very difficult!

I have even known people who have had their dog bite them for simply trying to put their dog's collar on, or when they have tried to remove their dog from their lounge chair, or take it out at night to go to the toilet.

Unfortunately, a lot of people out there have similar stories because their love for their dog is so great that they persist with behavioural problems, such as being dragged down the road each time they take their dog walking, or worse. You probably see this occurrence all the time, even in your own area.

In my opinion, there are three main reasons as to why people persevere with these problems:

a) they have become desensitised to the problem;

b) they love their dog no matter what; and

c) they probably don't realise that there is something you can do, with help available through their local dog training group, or through therapists such as myself.

I sometimes ask people why they persist with their dog and they say, 'because we couldn't imagine being without our dog, we love him'—and I'm sure this is true.

However, I have a suspicion that they don't consciously understand the real reason they persist. I think it has a lot to do with the fact that we often see our dogs as real family members and, as a son or daughter may do something wrong, no matter what it may be, they are still our children and part of us and we will defend them to the end, somehow justifying their actions.

How Denial can have Consequences

Anything we own or consider ours that we perceive to be of great value, we humans tend to protect and defend. The way many of us defend our dog's actions is no exception. For this very reason, I feel owners who cannot control or cure their dog's behavioural problems will invariably deny their severity or existence, often with many excuses. I hear them say such things as, 'Well, he's only fourteen months old and he's doing these things because he's still a puppy', or 'He just has a happy, excitable nature and that's why he jumps up on everyone'.

Many times I have called on a client, who has a dog that has bitten someone, to hear such things as, 'My son provoked Rover and that's why he was bitten'. I even had a lady say to me once (when her dog escaped out of her yard and ran up the road for about one hundred metres before biting a neighbour), that it did so because it must have thought someone was going to rob her house!

I am always cautious when arriving at a client's home and I'm told, 'You're alright John, my dog won't bite you'. I hear this sort of denial on a regular basis. Then if the dog does happen to bite someone, they will usually say something like, 'I can't understand it, he's never bitten anyone before'. I feel this response from owners is due to them feeling ashamed, consciously or subconsciously, of having a dog that could possibly bite. On the other hand, because it doesn't bite them, they have become too complacent and don't manage the situation with enough care and control.

Yes, to deny our dog's shortcomings is human, however, it is bad for us, and our dog, and can often be very dangerous. I think when we realise we have a problem and admit it, we are then closer to solving our dog's behavioural problems.

4

Training Techniques

Desire, Interest, Attention

When I am teaching a client how to interact or train their dog, they often say, 'John, it's really me you're training isn't it?' When I hear this, I usually smile and jokingly agree, 'Yes'.

The dog is often the more intelligent partner in this human-dog relationship. It already knows how to react to, or do most things we want it to do, it is really us who need to learn how to communicate with our dog to get it to do our bidding. So, we need to be trained even more than our dog.

So let's look at Whisper Motivational Training and see how easy and fast it is to teach our dog when we understand how.

Desire in Action

Because all creatures are different, their desires and needs are also different. What may be desirable to one dog, may be of no value to another. However, most dogs are food orientated and desire food greatly, such as tasty meat treats. The treats I find dogs like are liver, small pieces of devon and various other commercial products. You may have to try a number of different products to find the right treat for your dog.

Toys are another training tool that your dog may desire, for instance, the squeaky ones seem to be a favourite with many dogs.

Yes, it is very important to your relationship with your dog to find out what his desires are, because these desires will be the strong motivators that are essential to train your dog effectively and quickly.

Interest

Now we have found the desire that motivates our dog, we need to stimulate its interest in that motivator. A good way to increase our dog's interest in a food motivator is to use it as a treat when rewarding good behaviour. You can put several tasty tidbits in your pocket or in a bum bag, ready for when your dog deserves a reward.

Attention

Before we can teach our dog any exercise, we first need to attract its attention. We can do this by using our dog's name in conjunction with a treat.

Place your dog on a lead and have it on your left side. With the treat in your right hand, bring it down to your dog's nose, then as it smells the treat, bring the treat up and under your chin, at the same time saying your dog's name. When your dog looks at you, give it the treat. Repeat this action several times in the first session.

Now, our next session is going to be slightly different. Put your dog once more on the lead held in your left hand, then call your dog's name as you bring the treat (once again held in your right hand) down to your dog's nose and as it looks at you, bring it up to your face, saying, 'Bobby, look'. As soon as your dog looks at the treat under your chin, give it the treat and say, 'Good dog, Bobby'.

Repeat this exercise every day until each time you tell Bobby to look, he looks at you. You are then both ready to proceed to the next exercise.

To Reprimand or to Not Reprimand

If your dog is doing something that displeases you, often the best response is to ignore the behaviour. Ignoring bad behaviour and rewarding good behaviour can often be very effective. However, in a real world this is not always possible. The dog that is barking at three o'clock in the morning is very hard to ignore, especially if you or your neighbours have to get up for work the next day! So, for situations when bad behaviour from your dog cannot be overlooked, I have found a voice reprimand to be the best way of stopping a behaviour you do not want.

I use a special reprimand sound. This is the only noise I will ever make when I want a dog to stop certain behaviour. That sound is, 'Aah', and I repeat it twice, 'Aah aah'. It works marvellously. It may take your dog about two weeks in some cases to become sensitive to this sound and you need to keep saying it no matter what the response. Soon you will find that when you say this sound, your dog will understand what it is that you do not want him to do.

This is the way it works. All your commands are delivered in a soft, quiet whispered voice and your reprimands—'Aah aah'—are done in a firm, normal-pitched voice without shouting. When your dog stops the behaviour you don't want, you immediately praise it so your dog understands it is not itself you are reprimanding but the behaviour. Therefore, if your dog comes into the house and you do not want it to, instead of saying, 'Rover, outside', you simply say 'Aah aah'. If your dog barks, instead of shouting for it to 'shut up', you say, 'Aah aah' again and so on. By only using the one sound to reprimand, it is amazing how quickly your dog will learn—and don't forget to praise it once it stops.

Having had horses as a child, I learned early in life that animals would respond more favourably to certain sounds that we humans make if they were more in keeping with that animal's natural sounds. As a young boy, whenever I wanted to catch my horse, if loose in the fields, I would get some bread, place it flat on my hand and whinny like a horse. My horse would respond by whinnying back and then he would come up to me for the bread, whereby I would get hold of him by the mane and he would let me take control of him. My horse always responded best when I used this natural method.

This experience with horses helped me immensely when I started experimenting with sounds that dogs would respond to, some thirty years ago. I quickly found that dogs will take more notice of sounds that are closer to their species' natural sounds than anything else. If a dog is not happy with another dog or person that it feels it ranks above in the pecking order, or it feels superior to, it will often growl. This is the dog's way of reprimanding a subordinate. This is what we are doing when we use 'Aah aah'. It is a human sound that dogs relate to as a growl. I have often heard mothers and grandmothers saying to children, 'Aah aah—don't touch—naughty'. Where it has come from who knows! It may just come instinctively with some mothers. Anyway, it works and that is the most important thing.

One of my clients, who is a primary school teacher, is so committed to using this word that she told me of a situation where she was marking some homework for her pupils, with her head in a book, when a few of the children started talking loudly. As I had been doing some

Wolves will growl to reprimand a subordinate.

training with her dog, from pure habit of using 'Aah aah', she said to her pupils 'Aah aah' automatically. On looking up, the whole class was sitting up like a statue. She was amazed! Yes, it is a very powerful sound if used correctly and consistently, without using any other reprimand words. So stop saying things like, 'No', 'Don't' or 'Stop' and only use the 'Aah aah' sound to have a much better behaved pooch.

Sit

One of the most useful exercises we can teach our dog is to sit on command. Our dog cannot jump up on us, or our guests, whilst sitting. If, while out walking, your dog gets into the habit of sitting every time you come to a road, or if it escapes from your backyard, this simple exercise may one day save its life. Yes, teaching your dog to sit has many advantages in situations that crop up in every day life.

To commence, put your dog on the lead with it on your left side and its favourite treat in your left hand. Bring the treat to its nose. On smelling the treat, your dog will try to get it. As this happens, bring your hand up and back in a smooth motion approximately 40 cm above your dog's head. As its head goes back to follow the treat, its bottom will go down into a sit position. The instant this happens, give your dog the treat and say, 'Good dog'. Please note that the sit position should only be held for a maximum of two or three minutes.

Practice this exercise on the first session for about seven minutes, increasing the duration to ten minutes in the next session. Keep each session to ten minutes thereafter. This exercise needs to be done twice daily for four days. After this period of time, you should have perfected

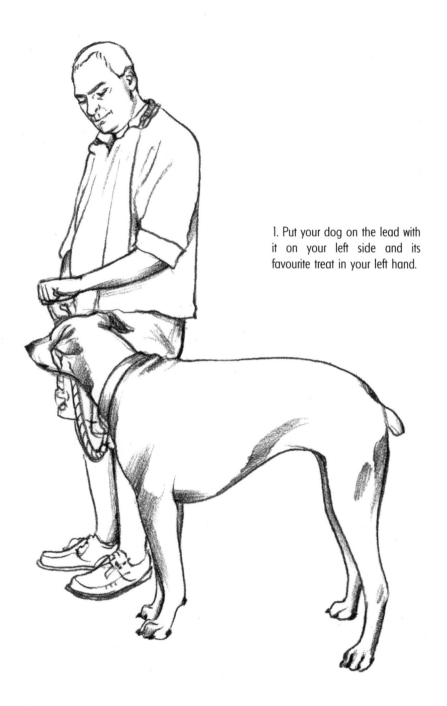

1. Put your dog on the lead with it on your left side and its favourite treat in your left hand.

this technique and your dog should be sitting with confidence each time you do this exercise. You are now ready to go on to the next stage—offering random rewards.

As before, have your dog on your left side, holding the treat in your left hand. Bring the treat down to your dog's nose and as it gets

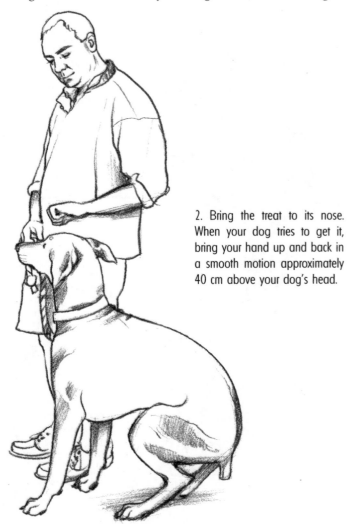

2. Bring the treat to its nose. When your dog tries to get it, bring your hand up and back in a smooth motion approximately 40 cm above your dog's head.

interested in the treat, bring it down slowly over its head. Because of the previous training in this exercise, your dog will sit straight away but instead of the treat, give your dog a soft pat and say, 'Good dog'. Repeat this exercise twice daily for two more days, sometimes giving your dog the treat and sometimes a soft pat, with praise.

3. As its head goes back to follow the treat, its bottom will go down into a sit position.

Voice Control

Now your dog is ready for you to introduce voice control. Commence the sit exercise as previously described. Bring the treat slowly over your dog's head and as you do so, say 'Sit' in a quiet whispered tone. As your dog sits, instantly give it the treat and praise it verbally with, 'Good dog'. All you need to do from now on is to randomly give the treat, (ranging from the second to the fifth time it sits on command). Whether you are using a treat or not, use the same hand gesture as you say 'Sit', ensuring that when you are not using a treat, your right hand is held in the same way as if the treat was in your hand. This gesture then becomes the hand signal for the sit command. Also remember not to say 'Sit' loudly, a whisper is all that is needed in conjunction with the reward and hand signal to get a perfect sit every time.

Down

The down exercise can be used in many everyday situations when we want our dog to stay for longer periods of time.

Place your dog on a lead on the traditional left-side position and have your dog sit as previously explained. As your dog sits, praise it, then holding a treat in your right hand, bring it near your dog's nose. Place your left hand on your dog's back and now slowly bring your right hand (which is holding the treat) down to the ground directly in front of it, at the same time guiding it gently down with your left hand. The moment your dog goes down, praise it and give it the treat instantly. At no time push your dog down with your left hand, as this simply makes it brace itself and it will not follow the treat to the ground.

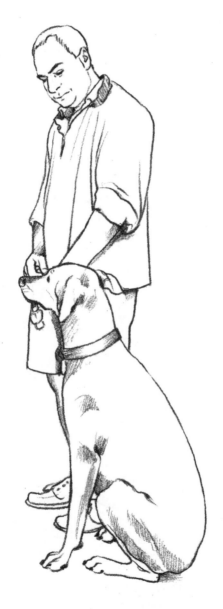

1. Place your dog on a lead on the left-hand side and have your dog sit.

Do this exercise twice daily for three days, then add voice control by simply saying 'Down' as your dog's body touches the ground, encouraging it down with the treat and guiding it down with your left hand. A whispered 'Down' is all that is required. Your hand gesture, as you move the treat forward, becomes your dog's signal to go down. This same signal is used whether you are holding the treat or not.

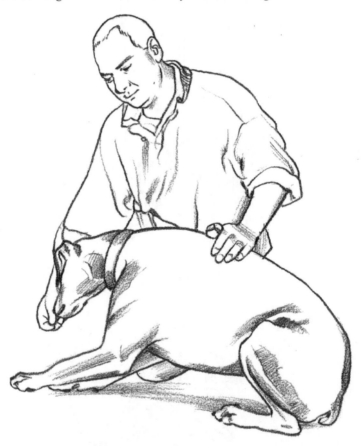

2. Place your left hand on your dog's back, slowly bring your right hand (holding the treat) down to the ground directly in front of it, guiding your dog gently down with your left hand.

Do not shout or push your dog down. If you are having difficulty with the down signal, just check your technique and go over each and every step carefully and try again with patience and persistence until you eventually succeed. Very soon you will have an obedient dog that will go into the down position every time you give the down command.

3. The moment your dog goes down, praise it and give it the treat instantly. At no time push your dog down with your left hand.

Recall

Many clients tell me that the most frustrating time they have with their dog is when they let it off the lead in their local park to run and play. Of course, this is the fun part of the outing. The problem begins when it is time to go home and their dog totally ignores whatever they do or say! So, the recall exercise is a must for dog owners.

The best place to start educating your dog on recall is in the home or in your own backyard, as here you have more control over your dog. Have your dog free, off-lead. Place a treat in your right hand and have a couple in your pocket. Do this, if possible, without your dog noticing. Now wait until your dog is not taking any notice of you and is away from you, then call its name followed by 'Come'. For example, 'Bobby, come'. As your dog approaches you, step backwards. A few steps are all that is necessary. Then bend down as your dog reaches you, give it the treat and make a fuss of it. Repeat this exercise several times each day until your dog is coming to you every time he is called. Once this happens start giving the treat at random—sometimes your dog gets it, sometimes it won't. However, your hand motion should always be as if you are holding a treat. When you are not using the treat you must pat and praise your dog when it reaches you.

Once your dog is coming to you when you call it on a regular basis, have it sit in front of you by doing the sit exercise, before giving it the treat. When this is working well for you, repeat the recall exercise in your backyard.

When your dog is coming to you in the house and backyard, then it's time to do the same exercise in the park. Initially go to the park at a quiet time so that distractions are at a minimum, then when your dog progresses, increase its exposure to distractions until your dog is coming to you no matter what is happening around you. Eventually you will be able to stop stepping backwards or bending down. You should only have to stand there and say, 'Bobby, come', and your dog will run to you. Another excellent way to improve your dog's recall is to raise your left hand above your head when recalling your dog, especially at a distance.

The repetition of mealtimes can also be used to help the recall exercise, whereby you call your dog to come when you are about to feed it. Wait until it is away from you, then call it to you, have it sit and give it its dinner.

I find clients who have the most problems with their dog not coming to them, have called their dog to come after it has done something that they disapprove of. When it has obediently come to the owner, they then reprimanded it by either shouting or smacking the dog. Dogs have long memories, and experiences such as this are not easily forgotten. When faced with this situation, you can't blame a dog for not coming to you when called. So, even if your dog eats your prize-winning roses, don't recall it to reprimand it. Always praise your dog when it comes to you, no matter what, and very soon the frustration of it not coming when off-lead will disappear.

Heeling at Whisper

As rules and regulations for dog owners increase and free off-lead areas are becoming scarce, a dog that walks quietly with us, on or off-lead, is a must. I have previously explained how to Whisper Walk with your dog in chapter two, and Heeling at Whisper is another version to teach a dog to walk quietly off-lead, as I have found some dogs respond to one method better than another.

First place a soft collar on your dog, then attach a short (80–100 cm) lead. I prefer a shorter lead to the traditional long lead as I notice my clients, when first learning to train their dog, find a shorter lead easier to handle. They say that they have enough to contend with already without the problem of reeling in a long lead, which is not necessary.

After attaching the lead (with your dog on your left hand side), bring it across the front of your body, from left to right, and hold it loosely in your right hand. Place a treat in your left hand and bring it down to your dog's muzzle (nose) with the knuckles of your left hand forward holding the treat in your fingers. Holding the treat in this position should immediately get your dog's attention. As this happens, step off slowly on your left foot, keeping your left hand slightly ahead of your dog. As it follows the treat, take only six to seven paces, then with your hand in the same position give it the treat. Continue this exercise four or five times in this first session.

At your next session, repeat the previous exercise until you have your dog competently heeling with you for six or seven paces, then increase the distance up to ten to fifteen paces, then fifteen to twenty paces. Once your dog is heeling by your left side for fifteen to twenty paces and staying close to your left side, you are ready then to do the heel and sit combination.

As before, have your dog on the lead on your left side with a treat in your left hand, knuckles forward. Now walk forward five to six paces, with your dog in the heel position. Come to a halt and by bending your left elbow up and slightly back, close to your left side, bring your left hand (still holding the treat) backwards over your dog's head, bringing it to a sit position. Give your dog the treat as it sits.

Step off again on your left foot and this time walk ten to fifteen paces before repeating the sit and reward exercise. At each and every session, increase the distance you heel your dog and every time you stop, have your dog sit and reward it with a treat. When you have perfected this exercise and your dog is heeling and sitting every time you stop, you will be able to progress to randomly treating your dog when heeling or sitting it and instead of a treat, simply give it a pat and praise it with a 'Good dog'.

When turning with your dog in a heel position, do this slowly at first until it gets used to turning, then if it lags behind, pat the top of your left leg briskly, saying at the same time, 'Come Rover'. This will encourage your dog to quicken its pace and as it does praise it and give it a treat. Once this exercise is going smoothly for you and your dog understands what is required for it to receive a treat, a pat or praise, it is time to add voice control.

Adding Voice Control

Providing your dog is now competently heeling with you and following your left hand (which is holding the treat), it is now time to whisper 'heel' as you step off on your left foot. On stopping, continue to bring your hand up (with the treat), as previously explained, encouraging your dog to sit and at the same time whisper 'Sit'. As your dog now knows what it needs to do to receive the treat, by adding the verbal commands it will soon relate the verbal stimulus to the actions of 'Heel' and 'Sit', enhancing its overall performance.

Once your dog has progressed to this level, it's now time to hold both the treat and the lead in your left hand. The lead should be held

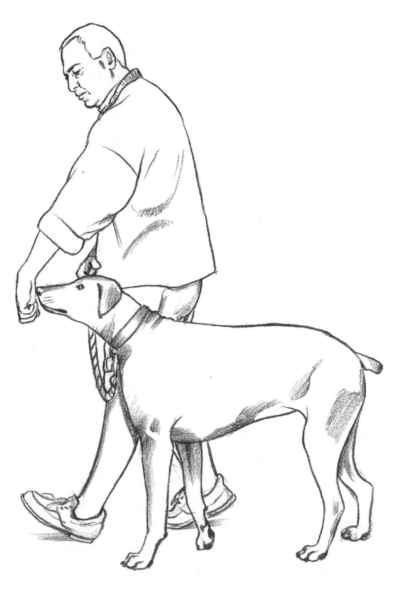

With your dog on your left hand side, bring its lead across the front of your body, from left to right, holding it loosely in your right hand. Bring your left hand (with treat) down to your dog's nose. Step off on your left foot, keeping your left hand slightly ahead of your dog. As it follows the treat, take only six to seven paces, then with your hand in the same position give it the treat.

approximately 50–60 cm above the collar (less for a large dog). By now your dog should have become accustomed to walking quietly by your side, and when you stop and sit it, you should continue to randomly give it a treat. Eventually the treat can be kept in your pocket or in a bum bag, and you will only need to occasionally produce a treat for it. By this time your dog will be heeling so close to you that people will think that your obedient dog is glued to your left leg!

Off-Lead Heeling

The feedback that I receive from dog owners, is that they would love to have a dog that they could control off-lead. My opinion is that anyone wanting off-lead control must first teach their dog to heel off-lead.

Prior to teaching your dog off-lead heeling, be sure your dog is now walking on-lead next to you without pulling. Put your dog on the lead, place some treats in your pocket or a bum bag and take it out into a quiet area, preferably an off-grass area, like a pathway, or a quiet street such as a cul-de-sac. Now walk your dog on-lead at a very slow pace for approximately fifteen to twenty minutes in a heel position. This will settle him down. Hold a treat in your left hand (as previously explained). Wait until your dog is walking by your side quietly and not looking at you, then very gently slip the lead over your dog's back and slowly bring your left hand holding the treat up to your stomach. Keep walking at the same pace for five or six steps, then calmly take the lead up in your hand again. At this point, put the slightest pressure on the lead so your dog knows you still have control, if you need it.

Continue this exercise until your dog stays by your side each time you slip the lead over his back. Then add voice control by saying 'Sit' when you stop, and if your dog moves ahead of you when the lead is over its back, get hold of the lead and place a little tension on it while saying 'Heel'. As it comes back into line with you, say 'Good dog', then bring the treat to its nose, attracting its attention. Give it the treat. Continue this exercise for a week, until it is walking nicely by your side while the lead is on its back.

Once you have reached this stage, in place of a lead, do this exercise with a light piece of string approximately 60 cm long. Attach the string to your dog's collar. Once your dog settles, instead of placing the lead over its back, put the string over its back, occasionally treating it as it walks quietly by your side. Sometimes give a little slight touch to the string, so your dog is now thinking that you always have some way of controlling it. Do this exercise for four to five sessions, then remove the string and just use your treat and voice control to have your dog heel by your side from now on.

Fetch Nicely

Imagine how much easier life would be if we had a dog that could find our mobile telephone or car keys every time we misplaced them. Well, to realise this very achievable goal, we first must teach our dog to retrieve.

Increasing the Chase Instinct

Certain breeds of dogs are more genetically predisposed to the chase instinct than others, however, it has been my experience that most dogs, no matter what their breed or mixture of breeds, usually have a healthy chase instinct lurking only slightly beneath their furry little coats. All that is required to achieve this is suitable motivation for our dogs.

Most dogs, no matter what their breed or mixture of breeds, have a healthy chase instinct.

To teach our dog to retrieve enthusiastically, we need to develop this natural chase instinct. We first need to select an article that will move quickly across the ground as a small animal in flight response might do. For this I find a soft ball to be most suitable. Start by tying your dog up close to where you are going to play, but not where it can reach you, and then commence playing ball. If possible, throw the ball against a wall, letting it bounce back. Now throw it along the ground. Laugh and run around with the ball. Enjoy! Have fun. If your dog gets excited, praise it and go over and give it a treat and a pat. Do this exercise for about five to ten minutes, then go inside and put the ball away. Let your dog off the tether and play with it, giving it lots of pats to make this a happy experience. Give it a treat. Do this exercise twice a day for four or five days and you should soon see your dog's interest in the ball growing in intensity. Once this happens, it's time to go to the next stage.

As before, have your dog tethered. Play with the ball but now, after about two minutes of play, put your dog on a long thin line and let it dangle on the ground. Release your dog from the tether and start throwing the ball around without your dog being able to get it, saying to your dog in a very excited manner, 'Rover, where's the ball? Where's the ball?' Roll the ball along the ground and as your dog runs after it, praise it as you pick up the end of the line. Walking forward, gather the line in your hands and on reaching your dog, praise it and pat it excitedly. Holding the end of the line, walk away still facing your dog. As you do, call it to you, saying, 'Rover, come', at the same time gently reeling it in as it approaches. Gently take the ball out of its mouth and immediately give it a treat and praise it. Repeat this exercise for several training sessions, then go to random treats, remembering that when no treats are offered, you must pat and praise it instead.

Adding Voice Control

As when teaching any training exercise, I only add voice control when I feel the dog totally understands what I want of it and is doing the exercise with confidence. I use voice control only as secondary stimulus, as I have seen too many people fail miserably when trying to get their dog to perform a particular task by using verbal commands, then repeating those commands over and over again, and getting frustrated or even angry, when their dog does not respond to their commands. As I mentioned previously, dogs are not the verbal communicators that we are. Initially, a word means nothing to a dog, it's only when a dog performs a particular action and a word is put to that action as a stimulus, that a dog relates to voice control.

Having succeeded in getting your dog to chase the ball enthusiastically, bring it back to you (and give it up), we now add voice control.

Have your dog sit on your left hand side. Now throw the ball and say in an excited manner, 'Rover, fetch'. As Rover fetches the ball, move away, walking backwards while still facing him, calling him to you saying, 'Rover, come'. When he reaches you, have him sit in front of you. Take the ball away from him, saying 'Out', and then immediately give him a treat. When not giving him a treat, give him a pat and say 'Good dog'. They say practice makes perfect. Well, in fact, it's perfect practice that makes perfect. So plenty of perfect practice will be needed to give you a perfect retrieving pooch.

Stand and Stay

One of our dogs' natural postures is to stand, so this is a relatively easy exercise to teach your dog and a very useful behaviour to be able to get your dog to do. You may not always want your dog to sit, but you may want it to stay in a stand position.

Walk your dog on-lead on your left side in a heel position, holding the lead in your right hand and anchoring it with your left hand close to the collar. Stop, and as you do so, place your right hand (palm facing inwardly) in front of your dog's nose, slightly touching its nose. Do this exercise several times until your dog is doing it correctly, then add voice control to the hand signal, saying, 'Stand stay'.

At first your dog may sit. If this happens, take one step forward, which will prompt your dog to stand again. Then holding the lead in your right hand close to the clip, put your left hand under your dog's stomach (near its stifle) and lift it to stop it from sitting, saying 'Stand stay'. Repeat the same exercise three times.

Once your dog is competent in the stand stay using the above method, return to holding your lead in your right hand and use the hand signal, as before, with your left hand to your dog's nose (palm facing inwards). Then, using voice control, say 'Stand stay'. Repeat this exercise several times for three days. By this time your dog should stand stay on command.

1. Stop after heeling for a while, holding the lead in your right hand, place your left hand (palm facing inward) in front of your dog's nose, lightly touching its nose.

2. If your dog sits, take one step forward, then holding the lead in your right hand close to the clip, put your left hand under your dog's stomach (near its stifle) and lift it to stop it from sitting, saying 'Stand stay'.

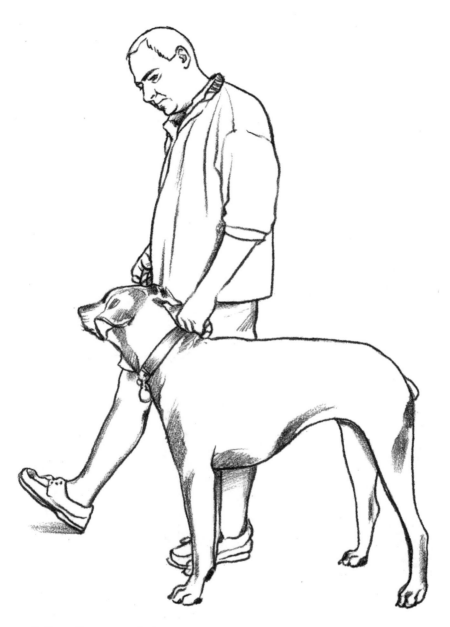

3. Step off on your right foot. Your dog will always be watching for your direction. By stepping off the foot furthest away from it (unlike heeling), it will indicate to your dog to remain still.

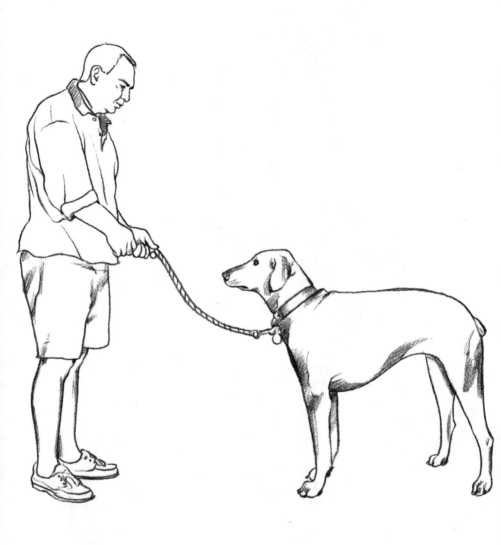

4. Swivel directly in front of your dog, pause briefly, then return to your dog's side. Try this a few times until it can stay for about one minute, then progress to step 5.

5 & 6 (see overleaf). Walk around your dog in an anti-clockwise direction (so you are actually walking behind it to come back to its right side).

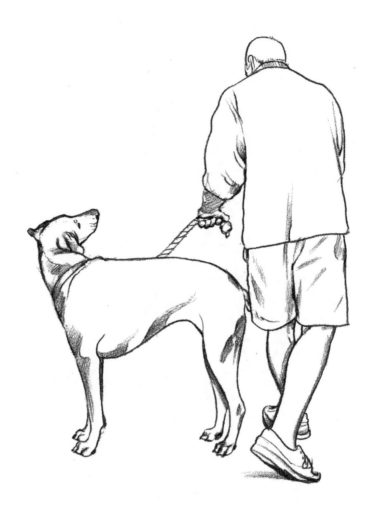

Stand for Inspection

This exercise is an extension of the stand stay exercise and is necessary for people who show or trial their dogs. It can also be used to control your dog from lunging at people and in any situation where your dog needs to be examined or restrained.

As before, have your dog on-lead on your left side. Stand stay your dog. Step off on your right foot and swivel directly in front of your dog. Remain there for 15 seconds, then return to your dog's side in a heel position. Do this several times until your dog will stand stay while you swivel in front of it.

Repeat this exercise, but as you stand in front of your dog, facing it, take one step backwards, holding the lead loosely in your left hand. There should be no tension on the lead. Now return to your dog and praise it, giving it one pat only. Do this exercise several times until your dog is competent, then repeat the exercise, however this time, after taking one step backwards, now go back to your dog in an anti-clockwise direction, holding a loose lead. Watch that you don't stand on your dog's tail, because if this happens, your dog will never be comfortable about this exercise and will be spooked every time you walk around behind it. Do this exercise several times for two to three days until your dog is performing this exercise correctly.

When your dog is up to this level, have a friend (who is familiar to your dog) hold your dog in a stand stay position, as you stand on your dog's left side. Starting at your dog's head, gently run your hands back, along the sides of its head, neck and then down its shoulders. As you do this, have your friend give it a treat. While you do this exercise, also have your friend quietly praise your dog in a whisper. Do this several times.

Repeat the exercise, but now run your hand from the sides of your dog's head, down its neck and down and up its shoulders, then right back and down its thighs. If it moves, simply ignore it and go back to only running your hand down its front end. Once your dog accepts you touching its head, neck and shoulders, gradually increase the area to include other parts of its body, until you are able to put your hands all over the dog without it cringing or moving.

The next step is to repeat the same exercise but using a stranger to hold the dog, instead of a friend.

Once you have accomplished this exercise you are now ready to go to the next stage which is approaching your dog from all angles, which a stranger or show judge may do. You should start by doing this exercise yourself, first coming towards your dog slowly from the left hand angle, then examining it, as before, then walking away and coming towards it from another angle. Eventually, you will be able to approach your dog from any angle—front, back, side—without your dog showing any discomfort or fear.

Then have a friend whom your dog knows, do the same exercise while you are holding your dog. Once your friend has got the dog to accept them with this exercise without shying away, then introduce a stranger to walk up and examine your dog in the same way from all angles. As before, use a treat and praise your dog each time it does not move or shy away from the stranger. Use no reprimand with this exercise. Reward what you want and ignore the behaviour you don't want. The exercise is learnt when you can put your dog in a stand stay position and anyone can come up and inspect it all over, without it moving or shying away or becoming aggressive.

Sit Stay

To be able to have your dog stay in a particular position for the length of time you choose, is very useful. You may want to put your dog in a sit stay when opening a gate, opening your front door, or when it tries to push its way into the house at your backdoor (which dogs often do). When taking your dog to the letterbox to get the mail or when meeting a friend in the street, it's nice to be able to get your dog to quietly sit and stay by your side. Yes, there are many situations on a daily basis where it's very useful to have your dog sit and stay.

To commence this exercise, place your dog on your left side on-lead, holding the lead in your right hand. Using a treat, as previously explained, sit your dog. Now place your left hand (palm facing inward) with the index finger pointing to your dog's nose. Slowly take one small step sideways away from your dog, then step back to your dog. Providing your dog doesn't move, give it a treat. If your dog moves, say 'Aah aah' and resit it.

Once your dog is doing this exercise correctly and not moving, increase the steps until you can eventually take three to four steps to the side without your dog moving. At this point, add voice control by pointing your left finger at your dog's nose as you say 'Stay'. Make sure you always have a loose lead in this exercise. Even a slightly tight lead will make your dog move, as it will confuse it. To your dog, a tightening of the lead means that you want it to follow you.

Front Step Out

Now instead of stepping out to the side of your dog, tell it to stay while pointing to its nose with your left index finger. Step off on your right foot, swivelling directly in front of your dog, pause briefly, then return to your dog's side. Providing your dog hasn't moved, give it a treat. Build this exercise up until your dog will sit and stay for approximately one minute.

Repeat the exercise as before, however, as you swivel, take one step backwards, pause, then return to your dog's side. Do this exercise several times, then do the same exercise but walking around your dog in an anti-clockwise direction (so you are actually walking behind it to come back to its right side).

Once your dog will sit and stay on a lead, repeat the same exercise but before leaving your dog, quietly drop the lead to the side and slightly to the back of your dog. Repeat this exercise twice a day for about three to four days.

Then include distractions. You could try to have someone bounce a ball near it. Also, someone could call to it while it is sitting and staying. Reprimand it with an 'Aah aah' if it moves and if it doesn't move, reward it with a treat. Keep doing this exercise until your dog will sit and stay under any circumstances.

1. Place your dog on your left side, on lead, in a sit position, holding the lead in your right hand. Place your left hand (palm facing inward) with the index finger pointing to your dog's nose.

2 & 3. Slowly take one small step sideways away from your dog, then step back
to your dog.

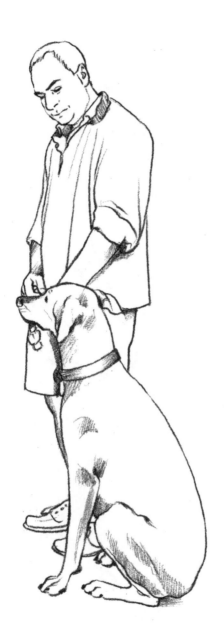

4. Step off on your right foot.

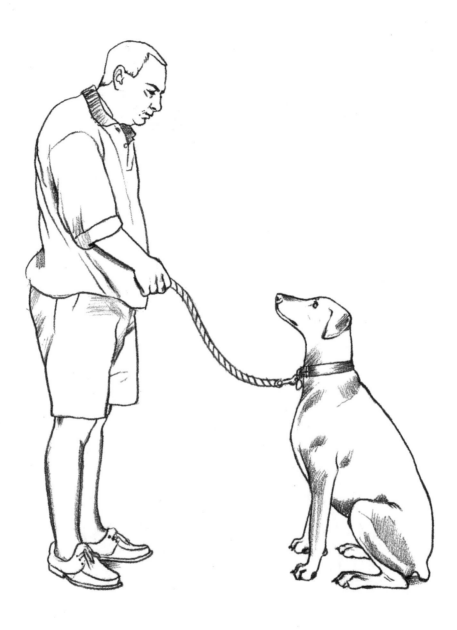

5. Swivel directly in front of your dog, pause briefly, then return to your dog's side. Try this a few times until it can stay for about one minute, then progress to step 6.

6 & 7. Walk around your dog in an anti-clockwise direction (so you are actually walking behind it to come back to its right side).

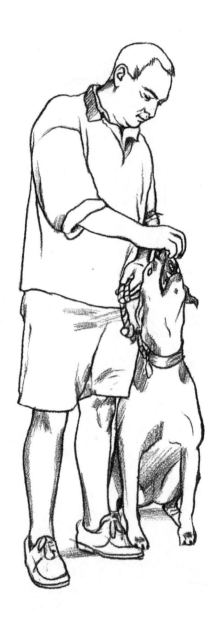

8. When your dog does the exercise correctly, reward it with a treat.

Down Stay

To be able to get your dog to lie down and stay there for any length of time has huge advantages in day-to-day situations.

I recently spoke to a client whom I had previously helped with some standard obedience training for his ten-month-old Rottweiler. This chap said that he was an enthusiastic surfer and would often go to Bondi Beach to ride the waves. He would place his towel with all his belongings on the sand, then put his Rottweiler, Bobby, into a down stay position near the articles. He said he would often go surfing for thirty to forty-five minutes and, on returning to the beach, his dog and belongings were always there.

Another client and his wife often visit their local restaurant for lunch on a Sunday and think nothing of leaving their seven-month-old German shepherd/husky-cross, Yo, at the door of the restaurant in a down stay position while they have lunch. They said that, providing no one steps on him as they come through the door, Yo stays lying there until they come out. I actually told them to be careful with this practice as it may be asking too much of such a young dog, but they assured me they were not because he never moves and they can keep an eye on him through the restaurant window.

In my opinion, the down stay is an excellent exercise to teach your dog and also one of the easiest. So let's take a look at the down stay.

Place your dog on lead, taking hold of the lead in your left hand about 30 cm away from the collar. Sit your dog, holding a treat in your right hand as previously explained. As your dog sits, reward it. Then take another treat in your right hand, bringing it close to your dog's nose, then take it down directly in front of it. You will find it will follow the treat down. As it reaches the ground, give it the treat and using your open right hand (with your palm facing inward) give it the stay signal. If your dog tries to get up, reprimand it with an 'Aah aah'. If it stays, reward it with a treat. Do this exercise three to four times for two days, then add voice control.

Put your dog in a sit stay as before. As it sits, give it a treat. Now, holding another treat (as before), bring it to your dog's nose and as you bring your right hand down holding a treat, add voice control by whispering 'Down'. As your dog reaches the ground whisper 'Stay'.

As you progress, take one step sideways holding a loose lead. Then come back to your dog. Providing it doesn't move, reward it with a treat. Do the same exercise, but increase the amount of steps to the side, up to three small steps. Practice stepping forward, as in the sit stay, by stepping off on your right foot and swivelling in front of your dog, then returning. Build this up until you can walk around your dog, clockwise and anti-clockwise, several times without it moving.

Once your dog is competent at this, repeat the same exercise but this time drop your lead and repeat the previous exercises without holding the lead. If your dog moves reprimand it with an 'Aah aah' but, of course, praise it when it stays. Practice this exercise twice a day for five days and you will soon have a staying dog you will be proud of.

Find It

One of the most bonding and pleasant exercises you can teach your dog is to find lost articles. At first, I like to teach this exercise in the home. For this task, it is easy to use your dog's dinner as the motivator. Put your dog's usual dinner in its bowl at mealtime. Place your dog on a lead. Have your partner, or a friend, hold it, then with bowl in hand, walk up to your dog and give it a couple of small pieces of its dinner from the bowl. Now, take its dish away and place it as far as possible within the house, but still within its sight. Place its bowl on the floor and have your accomplice let it go. As your dog goes to its meal, which it will do enthusiastically, praise it. Repeat this exercise three to four times, then let your dog finish its dinner.

At the next session, do the exercise in the same way but now place the bowl in another room out of its sight before having your accomplice release your dog, while saying, 'Find'. Do this new version again three or four times at mealtimes for four days, then stop using an accomplice and instead of your dog being held, tie it up. Take its food into another room out of its sight. Return and release it, placing your hand over its muzzle (so it gets used to finding an article with your scent) and whisper 'Find'. Soon this will be a game it will love. When this happens, and this should only take a few days, you can do this exercise at times other than mealtime, substituting the dog food for a few treats. First tie your dog up and give it a treat, then let it see you put a few treats in the bowl. Next, place the bowl with the treats in another room, out of its sight, return to your dog and on releasing it, whisper 'Find', placing your hand over its muzzle at the same time.

Once your dog is doing this part of the exercise correctly, progress to other objects. An old worn sock of yours turned over a few times, or some similar item, can be a good 'find' article.

Tie your dog up and put the sock in the dish with a treat under it. Place the sock in such a way that it must remove the sock to get the treat. Now go back to your dog, place your hand over its muzzle, release it and say 'Rover, find' as you follow it, walking towards its bowl. When your dog reaches its bowl, it will have to remove the sock to get to the treat As soon as this happens, praise it. After completing this successfully a few times, repeat the exercise but now omit the treat. When your dog approaches the dish with the sock, it will most probably remove the sock to check for treats. In this case, as soon as it touches the sock say 'Good dog', and give it a treat from your hand.

The next step is to do exactly the same exercise as above but to stop using the bowl and just use the sock for your dog to find. Release it and as explained previously, follow it as it reaches the desired destination. On touching the sock, praise it excitedly saying 'Good dog', and give it the treat.

Next start hiding the sock, first in easy to find places then slightly harder and finally more difficult to find places. Once this is successfully achieved, start replacing the sock with other articles of yours—a mobile telephone, keys, your watch—the list is endless. You will soon appreciate the pleasure of having a furry friend that can find almost anything.

Motor Manners

Even if your dog does not frequently accompany you on car journeys, some learning of basic car manners is needed. After all, dogs require regular veterinary checkups at least once a year, and most owners will take their dog by car. There are also the occasions when you are going away on holidays and your dog either comes with you, or needs to be driven to the kennels. So, it makes good sense to spend some time on your dog's motoring manners.

First of all, make sure you have a good dog safety harness and secure it to the back seat of your car, both for your dog's safety and your own. Always use a harness when your dog is in the car, even for short trips.

Place your dog on a short lead of approximately 80 cm in length and walk it to the passenger side back door of your car. (I find this to be the safest place for your dog to enter or alight, because when you pull up to the kerb on your passenger side, you are able to open your back door without fear of either the door or your dog being hit). Have your dog sitting in such a position that it will not have to move when you open your car's back door. Open the door holding your dog's lead loosely in your right hand (and it is a good idea to have a few treats in your pocket). Step into the back of your car and encourage your dog to join you. If it does, treat and praise it. Now secure the harness and reward it with another treat.

When arriving at your destination, open the rear passenger door. If your dog starts to move, reprimand it with an 'Aah aah' and 'Stay'. Unfasten its harness and get it to step down out of the car and as soon as its paws touch the ground, say 'Sit stay'. Reward your dog when it does. Have it sit until you are ready to move off.

There are three things you definitely need when taking your dog out in the car—control, control and more control! This technique is the best way to achieve this.

Car Phobia

Some dogs just can't wait to get into a car and go for a ride, but there are others that simply don't like it at all. These dogs will often struggle and make a fuss, so some gentle persuasion is needed.

Desensitising

Have some of your dog's favourite treats in your pocket or bum bag, then position your car in your driveway (or an area where you can open all doors with safety). Place your dog on a long lead (approximately 1.8 m) and take it to the car. If it hesitates and starts to pull as you near the car, let it go to the end of the lead, as this will make it feel more at ease. However, keep bringing your dog in gently to the car so that it is close enough to enable you to sit on the front passenger seat with your legs still outside the car and your feet touching the ground.

By now your dog will probably be as far away from the car as the lead will allow. If so, start encouraging it closer to the car using its favourite treats. Do this exercise for two to three days, first throwing the treat to your dog's distance, then hold the treats out to your dog until it is coming right up to the car for them. Do this several times, then, with all the car doors open, start throwing a treat up to the car, then into the car. Try the front passenger side first, then the back.

Play this game for five days, throwing the treats into the car, having your dog jump in to get them. Once your dog is comfortable getting into the car on its own, get into the car yourself, still with all the doors open and call it to you. Do this for three days, until your dog will willingly join you in the back of the car. Then continue with this exercise, but with the front driver's side door closed. Once your dog is doing this exercise with one door closed, then close each of the other doors, one at a time, as your dog progresses. Soon you should be getting your dog in and out of the car with ease.

Once this is achieved, put your dog in the car and start the motor, running it at first for only a few seconds, then slowly building the time until you are able to run the motor for three to four minutes without your dog becoming anxious. Remember to reward for good behaviour and ignore the bad.

When your dog will get into the car and not panic when you run the engine for a few minutes, then it is time to drive your dog slowly up and down the road. Do this twice a day for three days, then progress to driving around the block for another three days. Providing this is going well, increase the distance gradually. Be patient, and within a few weeks your dog should be asking you to take it for a ride! There are also some natural remedies for dog car sickness and some of these may help if used in conjunction with desensitising.

The Barking Baritones

Wolves rarely bark. However, they do howl, especially when communicating at a distance. In many instances in the past, humans have found it beneficial to have a dog that would bark to warn them of danger and to keep predators away, or to round up sheep and cattle. For these and many other reasons, humans were pleased to have a companion that would bark. In fact, it was so favoured that humans selectively bred dogs to bark. However, in an urban community, a nuisance barker is now frowned upon and dogs create more trouble for themselves by barking than any other behaviour.

Barking is a large part of a dog's natural behaviour, but it is something we humans can find extremely irritating. It is also the major complaint that most councils receive, prompting them to now charge dog owners hefty fines for nuisance barkers. So how do we go about stopping our dog doing this agonising behaviour that we just can't stand?

We first need to know a little about the causes for our dog's barking which can occur for a number of reasons. Dogs can bark when wanting to come inside—this is attention-seeking. They can bark to warn off intruders—this is usually territorial. The dog's environment may be causing boredom or stress and this can give you a chronic barker. The list is long.

The only way you will successfully stop your dog from barking without it suffering side effects, is to take away the reason for it barking in the first place. Remove your dog's motivation to bark and you are 90 per cent of the way to alleviating the problem.

If your dog is bored, simply enhancing its environment could improve the barking situation. If your dog stands outside and barks to be let in, and you let it in, it will very quickly learn that it gets what it wants from barking. If your dog runs to the front fence and barks at a dog that is being walked, then cover the fence so your dog cannot see out. If your dog barks when guests call, tie it up when they are expected, then when they arrive, have them throw it a treat (from a distance). Very soon your dog will be wagging its tail in a friendly manner every time your friends call. Yes, take away the motivation and the problem is almost solved.

Now for the other 10 per cent of this equation. When your dog barks, reprimand it with voice control, saying 'Aah aah' in a higher tone, but not shouting (otherwise it will think that you are joining him in the barking and that is definitely a reason to keep going!) Then as soon as the barking stops, say 'Good dog'. The only time that you don't reprimand your dog for barking is when it is attention-seeking, such as barking directly at you to throw its ball, or when it wants a treat. This attention-seeking behaviour should be completely ignored.

Speak on Command

As I write this, I can't help thinking of a client, whose Siberian husky greeted me verbally in an almost human way as I approached their front door, with an 'Aroow aroow' (sort of a talking low-pitched howl). I thought at the time that if the owners wanted their dog to verbalise on command, this would be an interesting sound for their dog to make on cue.

To have your dog speak (bark) when asked, is also an excellent behaviour to teach your dog and has many benefits. Security is one such situation that comes to mind, especially if you have a dog that is more inclined to lick people than bark at them. If you are at home alone, it's a good deterrent to have a dog that will bark on cue. Imagine an elderly person who lives alone and has a fall, unable to reach the telephone. This could be a way of attracting a neighbour's attention to alert them that something is wrong, especially if the dog does not normally bark unless there is a reason.

A further advantage of this command is that it can also be used to control nuisance barking in some instances because, as well as teaching your dog to bark on cue, you can also teach it to stop barking with a stop command.

Before commencing this exercise, have some treats in your pocket and choose a word for the barking behaviour. I use 'Talk' together with my dog's name, for example, 'Rover, talk'. The introduction of a hand signal is also an advantage, as this allows you to ask your dog to bark without you actually having to speak to it.

Identify a situation which stimulates your dog to bark. It may be at the neighbour's cat, or when your dog wants food. When your dog starts to bark, say, 'Rover, talk' and at the same time use a subtle signal such as rubbing your chin. Make sure, though, that the gesture is a conscious action and not one you have acquired as a personal habit, otherwise your dog will be barking continuously! As your dog barks, reward it with a treat and once you want it to stop barking, say, 'Finish'. If it continues to bark after you have said 'finish' reprimand it with an 'Aah aah'.

Once you have this behaviour under control, you can advance by holding up one finger for one bark, two fingers for two barks, three fingers for three barks, and so on.

So the exercise would go as follows. You would say, 'Rover talk', hold up one finger and as soon as your dog barks once say, 'Finish'. If you dog continues to bark, you reprimand it with an 'Aah aah'. It only receives the treat when it barks once, when you hold up one finger. Continue with the exercise with one finger until it is competent with this, then progress to two fingers, eventually going up to five fingers for five barks. Then make the commands randomly—sometimes one, sometimes five fingers and only reward the correct response. The exercise requires a lot of patience and practice but is well worth the effort. This is what we call shaping a behaviour.

Shaping

At different stages of a dog's training (operant conditioning) it is often necessary for us to shape a behaviour in order for us to achieve our exact goals. Shaping is simply breaking up an exercise into small components to work on them. Let's say we are teaching our dog to retrieve a ball. We throw the ball and our dog runs off, picks up the ball and returns it to us, but then drops it at our feet. The behaviour we actually wanted is for it to fetch the ball, bring it to us and sit with the ball in its mouth in front of us until we say 'Out', and then give it up. To achieve this, we must teach the last part of this exercise first and then reward the correct behaviour.

Start by giving your dog the ball to hold in its mouth, then take hold of the ball and say, 'Out'. Have a treat in your hand and show your dog the treat. As it releases the ball, say 'Good dog' and give it the treat. Once this portion of the exercise is learned, give it the ball as before, but now step backwards a few paces and call it to you, 'Fido, come'. As your dog reaches you, give it the command to 'Sit' and as it sits, say, 'Good dog'. Then take hold of the ball and say 'Out'. When it gives up the ball, say, 'Good dog'.

Once this exercise is learned thoroughly, throw the ball and say 'Fido, fetch'. As your dog takes hold of the ball, step backwards a few paces calling it and encouraging it to you. When it reaches you, say, 'Sit', then as it sits, say, 'Good dog'. Then take hold of the ball and say 'Out' and give it a treat. Continue with the verbal encouragement and stepping backwards, until all you need to do is to throw the ball, stay where you are, and say, 'Fido, come'.

When your dog is fetching the ball to you, then sitting in front of you and giving up the ball when asked, you have successfully shaped the behaviour.

Positive Reinforcement

By using positive reinforcement we increase the chances of a particular action occurring again. For this technique to work we need to use a reward that the dog wants. The more it wants the reward, the better the chances are that positive reinforcement will have your dog repeating the action you are training it to do. I have found such things as food, toys, play and affection to be excellent tools to use when applying this method. When you ask your dog to sit and it does so, you give it a reward. You call your dog to come to you and when it does, you give it a pat. In both of these cases you have positively reinforced that behaviour. However, for your dog to associate the action with the reward, it must be given the reward the instant the action is done. If your response is some seconds later, it is too late. Timing is extremely important when using this powerful training principle.

5

Dogs—The Ultimate Helpers for Humans

Dogs of Force

Throughout the world, dogs are schooled in the fine art of detection, tracking and apprehending law-breakers. These dogs have proven to be an enormous help to law enforcement agencies in their day-to-day struggle to keep crime under control. The New South Wales Dog Squad is one such agency that is successfully using dogs' many natural skills and senses to their full advantage.

I was recently invited to their headquarters to have a first-hand and close-up look at these magnificent creatures in action. The Police Dog Unit was first started in 1932 with two German shepherds named Tess and Zo, and a constable by the name of Scott Denham was their handler. This unit was set up mainly for detection of offenders and missing persons. Tess and Zo are now immortalised in the Police Museum in Phillip Street, Sydney. This unit was disbanded in 1953 and there was no police dog unit in New South Wales until 1978, when Sergeant Robert Northcott and First Class Constable Graham Farrel travelled to Victoria and brought back the foundation members of the present squad, Rip and Cain, two male German shepherds, with the right temperament for police work.

Male German shepherds were predominantly used by the unit until 1989, when it was becoming increasingly difficult to find enough males that were suitable for police work. In total, only one dog in a hundred is accepted as a police dog as these dogs must be exceptional. A police dog has to be able to play safely with children one moment, without any fear of the slightest roughness or aggression, then in the next instant, switch to being a fierce law-enforcer, an extremely hard feat for any creature. The main reason for initially using only male German shepherds was size, as a male is usually bigger and heavier, seen as being more intimidating than a female because of this. This physical presence can be a psychological advantage when trying to get a law-breaker to surrender. However, once tried, it was discovered that the ladies proved to be a force to be reckoned with, as found with the first recruited female police dog, Sage. Sage was a little lady with a nice disposition but with a lot of fire in her tail if it was needed. She later went on to be a proud mother of four police dogs.

The Police Dog Unit was first situated at St Ives, a northern Sydney suburb, and then attached to the Goulburn Police Training Academy, not far south of Sydney. In 1998, the unit was again moved to Menai, a southern suburb of Sydney, where an excellent facility was established. Today both male and female German shepherds are still used extensively to fight crime, however, light, agile Rottweilers have now also been included in the squad. Rottweilers are particularly useful in siege situations because of their great jaw power and the ability to hang on to whatever, or whoever, they take hold of. This has proven to be a great asset to police in this type of situation.

Training includes firearm testing, when these dogs must hold steady under fire. They need to be hunters and have a good chase instinct, together with the persistence to reach the goal. The German shepherds and Rottweilers must be play orientated, because play is used as the reward in this branch of dog work. These dogs are well schooled with operational standard training of sixteen weeks, which includes obedience and agility. They then receive a further sixteen weeks in advanced training which includes tracking, detection and apprehending suspects. The tracking training starts with searching property and buildings, then the dogs progress to outdoor work. As the skills of the dogs increase, more obstacles are placed in their path.

Police unit dogs are also given plenty of opportunity to socialise in day-to-day situations, for instance, in crowded places, on boats, and crossing bridges, so that they become very familiar with all types of environments in their everyday work. In many cases, scenarios are set up to simulate crime scenes where a call will go out and an officer and his canine partner will race to the scene. On arriving, they might encounter a break-and-enter in progress in a warehouse, or a similar situation. In this way, the response of the dog and handler can be observed and assessed, with feedback given to improve the team's effectiveness. With each drill, the bond between the team becomes stronger, and the handler learns to read the dog's body language.

The dog handlers are also carefully selected, with the prerequisite being that these officers be experienced, with the ability and temperament to work alongside their canine partner. They need to be very fit, as this type of work can be extremely physical.

Merlin and his handler Senior Constable Matt McCaldie.

When I visited the dog unit, I was given a demonstration by Merlin and his handler, Senior Constable Matt McCaldie. Merlin was amazing and obedient—jumping over hurdles on command, climbing up a step ladder, negotiating narrow simulated bridges, and crawling through tunnels. Merlin was a happy dog and had no signs of stress whatsoever. He was extremely relaxed in his work and it was clear to see that he loved and respected his human partner. Interaction such as this, between human and dog, is an absolute joy to see.

Another popular breed now used by the unit is the labrador. These intelligent dogs, with their incredible sniffing capabilities, are used for drug and bomb detection. One very talented labrador was also trained to detect microlitres of accelerant in drums of fuel at fire scenes, for the New South Wales Fire Brigade. More dogs are to be trained for this type of work in the future.

Training for these dogs is very specialised indeed, and it has to be, as the work they carry out in the field is demanding and accuracy is everything. Sniffer dogs are fed their meals in two halves, only during training sessions, which are carried out twice daily. They are rewarded with small parts of their meal each time they find drug or bomb material successfully. The contraband is hidden inside objects that the trainer makes increasingly difficult for the dog to find. As the labrador is extremely food oriented (and many a labrador owner would vouch for that!), their dinner is their best reward. Only when their nose is successful will they be able to eat their meal. No wonder these dogs' searching skills are so acute. While visiting the police unit, I was given a demonstration of these dogs in action and was totally amazed at the accuracy they showed in detecting various drugs and bombs.

In this exercise, drug and bomb material is concealed inside a tin punctured with pinholes.

The German Shepherd

A large, angry dog commands respect, and if that dog is a German shepherd, skilled in the art of police work, then it most certainly should be respected and feared by the crooks and law-breakers of this world.

In many countries, this large, attractive dog is the breed most favoured by dog owners. As a boy in England, my Uncle Joe had a beautiful German shepherd called Lassie, which he identified as an Alsatian. Uncle Joe told me that the breed had come into England after World War I and that they were initially described as German shepherds. However, at that time, the English Kennel Club did not want any breed names obviously associated with Germany, so they renamed the breed, Alsatian, from their origins in the Alsace. This name remained until after World War II when the breed name once more reverted to German shepherd.

These highly intelligent animals have proven their outstanding ability in many roles, in many countries, as police dogs, guide dogs for the visually impaired, in search and rescue missions, and in assisting people with a disability. This breed is also used in all the armed forces.

Black and tan would have to be the most popular colour for this breed. My own German shepherd, Duke, was mostly black with a small amount of dark tan colouring, however, the colours I mainly see in the breed these days show a more even ratio of black to light tan. The colour range available is specified as dark, grey sable, bicolour, paled black and gold, black and fawn, and black. I have also seen a few white German shepherds in my time.

The size of a male German shepherd is approximately 63.5 cm high at the shoulder, with a weight of 34–38 kg, while bitches are approximately 58 cm high, with a weight of 27–31.5 kg.

As many of you will know, the German shepherd is also a good family dog and companion which will usually bond strongly with one family member. If that person has the time and ability to train and care for that dog, then the family will have a loyal and faithful best friend.

The Rottweiler

This canine body-builder, with its magnificent muscular and noble appearance, has played an important role throughout history in its interactions with humans. The origins of these dogs go as far back as the Roman Empire, where they were successfully used in battle. The Rottweiler has also been a competent cattle dog and was even used for bear hunting during the Middle Ages.

Rottweilers were brought to Germany by the invading Roman Army, who left many behind, to the delight of local butchers in Rottweil (Württemberg, West Germany), who used them to pull their carts because of their strength. Therefore, the name 'Rottweiler' originated from its days of toil in this region. In fact, natives of this area call them 'Metzherhund' (Butcher Dog). Butchers were known to tie their money belts around their dog's neck for safekeeping when going out to do business. Hence, they were never robbed.

An extremely intelligent dog, its instinctive guarding nature has been used to advantage by armies and police forces in many parts of the world. A Rottweiler's height ranges at the shoulder from approximately 25–27 cm for males and 23–25 cm for bitches. The male weighs approximately 52–61 kg and a bitch weighs 41–49 kg. A loyal and faithful dog, the Rottweiler makes a great guard dog for your family, but training and education is a must for this noble giant.

The Guide Dog

I met up with Jim and his guide dog, King, a three-year-old golden labrador, when travelling home by train from the city one afternoon. Although Jim is blind, both he and his dog looked quite relaxed and at ease with each other. I was impressed to see such a well-behaved dog in these circumstances, as most of the dogs I see on my daily rounds to clients are hyperactive and I'm sure, in this situation, would not be able to stay still. This golden 'gentleman' was patiently lying at Jim's feet without a murmur, looking as though he had not a care in the world. Jim and I began chatting about guide dogs. Jim told me that he and King worked as a team and this enabled him to be self-reliant.

A guide dog's life is one of dedication, loyalty and companionship. Starting off their preparation at eight weeks, they are exposed to as many noises and distractions as the world can offer. This is done by caring volunteers, known as 'puppy walkers', who also socialise and introduce guide dogs-in-waiting to manners and basic obedience. When out and about, these puppies wear a little dog coat with an 'L' on their back, so the public know that they are little learners! Their exposure to the environment encompasses rides on buses and trains, trips in taxis, visits to crowded busy streets and shopping centres and negotiating escalators. They are also socialised with dogs and humans up to the age of twelve to fourteen months, staying with their carers until their official guide dog training commences. A guide dog can still be effectively working until ten years of age, or older, in some cases.

I am told the hardest thing to do when placing a dog, is to be able to match the dog with the owner, as this union is virtually a marriage, and as we know, sometimes even human marriages can be difficult!

Jim told me that guide dogs work on command, so the more competent the owner is with directions, the more effective the team will be. He said that he, personally, found trains more user-friendly than any other public transport, as the carriages are suitable for a person with a guide dog to sit comfortably, with the dog at their feet.

When Jim is planning a train excursion, he walks to his local railway station, guided by King. Then it's over to Jim to work out which train he wants to catch. When that train pulls up and Jim hears it stop, he gives the command 'forward' to King. King then moves forward to the edge of the platform and stops, then, providing Jim is sure of the situation (which he may check with his white cane), he tells King to go 'forward' again. On entering the train, King is then told to find a seat.

Once this mission is accomplished, King is then asked to lie down until the train reaches his destination, when the same procedure is repeated in reverse order.

When this was explained to me, I felt a lump in my throat. It was touching to hear about a dog and a human working together so closely in this extremely worthwhile way, as such an effective, unified team.

King is Jim's second guide dog. His previous dog was just retired at fourteen years of age. In contrast to King, Pacer is a black labrador, understandably suffering a few ailments, but now he is retired, is able to quietly wander around Jim's home taking it easy. Jim said that both of his dogs are his best mates, but admits he has a soft spot for his old faithful mate, Pacer.

Now that King has taken over the guiding role, he is Top Dog and, even though it is early days in his career, he's handling it well, rising to the enormous task and responsibility of guiding Jim wherever he goes.

Jim says that even though a guide dog is a companion, first and foremost it is a working dog that has been trained to a high degree of obedience to enable it to perform its duties. Guide dogs work on command and are praised as a reward. It is important Jim maintains King's training, as his very life may depend on King's obedience.

There was also one very important piece of information Jim shared with me—if you encounter a guide dog, you should not pat or encourage it, as this can be detrimental to its training. The offering of food is also a 'no-no' as this can take the dog's mind off its work, perhaps having serious consequences.

Guide dogs here and overseas are helping people like Jim to lead a normal and productive life. To a person without sight, they are a guiding light.

Jim and King on the train. Guide dogs here and overseas are helping people like Jim to lead a normal and productive life.

The Labrador

Originally from Newfoundland, this gentle retriever can equip itself equally as well in either a working environment as a guide dog, working with police and customs officials to sniff out drugs and explosives, as a guard dog, a competent gun dog and hunter or as a faithful family dog that is extremely good with children.

Not lacking intelligence, the labrador has a strong, sturdy body that needs plenty of exercise and regular training. Anyone who owns one will tell you that they are good eaters, which means they can sometimes become overweight as they get older. Care must be taken to ensure they are not over-fed. Their intelligence, together with the fact that these dogs are so food oriented, makes them ideal for training in their particular working environment. A labrador will do almost anything for food, and clever tasks are achieved when the reward comes as a food treat.

The height of a male labrador ranges from approximately 54–62 cm and for bitches, approximately 54–59 cm. A male weighs approximately 25–34 kg and a bitch weighs approximately 25–31 kg. Labradors come mainly in black, brown or gold.

The Golden Retriever

Movie-star looks with a gentle touch is an apt description of this gentle giant, making them a favourite pet, especially with families with small children. This is a powerful dog with a beautiful coat requiring regular maintenance; an intelligent dog with a definite aim to please. An excellent retriever and hunter, this breed's sporting career was developed in England, however, the golden retriever's ancestors were sheep dogs that tended sheep in Russia.

Height for the male is approximately 58.5–60 cm at the wither, and for bitches approximately 53–58.5 cm. Weight is approximately 29.5–34 kg for a male and 27–32 kg for bitches.

Chariots of Speed

For a period of time, when I was growing up, I lived near our local greyhound racetrack. Many nights I sat on our back steps and watched these slender speed machines race enthusiastically around the track, fascinated at how fast these dogs could run with what seemed like effortless grace. Writing this book gave me the opportunity to delve into their origins and to learn as much about them as possible.

Throughout history, greyhounds have been companions to the rich, famous and have even been owned by royalty. This breed goes as far back as ancient Egypt, where Cleopatra found them delightful companions and hunting partners. Christopher Columbus thought them such an asset when visiting far off lands that greyhounds accompanied him on board when he embarked on his second expedition to the New World in 1493. Few people would realise that Australia's first imported dogs were greyhounds, arriving with Governor Phillip on the First Fleet in 1788. The greyhound is so special it is even mentioned in the Bible.

Greyhounds were originally developed for hunting rabbits and deer, although these days they are bred with speed in mind, for the modern pastime of greyhound racing.

In days gone by greyhound racing was often referred to as the 'poor man's sport' however, this has changed greatly with big prize money available for dogs with exceptional ability. In Australia, dogs can earn a fortune and large stakes are now on offer in events such as The Golden Easter, The Melbourne Cup, Australia Cup and Spring Stakes.

Greyhounds start their racing education at about twelve months of age with four to six weeks training, learning to catch the hare and to rail. After having a few months off the scene, they actually start racing at about sixteen months, often ending their career at around four years

Racing greyhounds can earn big prize money.

of age (excluding any injuries). On retiring, greyhounds are sometimes rehoused by greyhound adoption agencies, who assess them and arrange their adoption with suitable carers.

One thing that surprised me about greyhounds was their soft manner with humans. I suppose the reason for being surprised was that every time I had seen someone walking greyhounds in the street over the years, the greyhounds had always worn wire muzzles. However, I have since learned that the reason greyhounds are required to wear a muzzle in public is because they are natural hunters. This breed is what is called a sight hound, named appropriately because they hunt their prey mainly by sight rather than by tracking it down by scent. This is why the greyhound is so keen to catch that elusive hare! So rabbits, or cats, or even small dogs could be at risk as the greyhound sees them as fair game, hence the muzzle.

The Greyhound

The greyhound is a low maintenance dog that loves to socialise. It is usually calm and majestic in its manner—with an air of nobility in its own way. Most are very sensitive dogs that will take all the love and attention you can give them. In the main, these magnificent 'chariots of speed' are very special, gentle creatures.

A female greyhound weighs approximately 26 kg and a male up to 38 kg. Weight in racing is extremely important, as the scales cannot vary more than one kilogram from the greyhound's last start. A male's height is approximately 70 cm and a female approximately 65 cm. A greyhound can reach speeds of up to 60 km/h and apart from the cheetah, the greyhound is the fastest animal on land. Their short hair may be almost any colour, despite the breed's name.

Dogs in the Pest Control Industry

Many people who own cocker spaniels will be able to tell you of the virtues of this medium-sized charmer with a cute smile, cheeky, almost human, grin and brilliance in retrieving, if introduced to it correctly.

Some lateral thinkers in the pest control industry overseas, and now in Australia, are teaming up with this delightful little fellow in their fight to detect hard-to-find termites—and they are achieving amazing results.

I recently spoke to a leading pest control owner, Shane, who was using an eight-year-old golden cocker spaniel, Alf, for termite detection. Shane told me he had acquired Alf from a friend as a four-year-old. The friend had trained Alf using similar techniques developed for bomb detection in Ireland. Alf had been taught, in play, to retrieve pieces of conduit with termites blocked inside, and once this smell was imprinted, he was taken to real life situations for many hours of practical training.

On one occasion, Alf was asked to find a termite nest in an old bank building which was adjacent to other old shops that had been having problems with termites. None could be found, but while searching the bank building, Alf kept wanting to run outside to an old tree. Shane kept calling him back into the bank building to try to keep his nose right there, but Alf persisted in going back to the old tree, scratching furiously at the trunk. Eventually, Shane went with Alf's determination and found a large nest of termites in this old tree that were travelling underground into the bank building. Another case solved.

Alf has an approximate ten to fifteen-hour working week, sniffing out hard-to-find termites. His success rate is excellent, often finding a nest or sub-nest that has not been discovered by more conventional

Some lateral thinkers in the pest control industry are now using cocker spaniels to detect hard-to-find termites, such as Shane and his 'detective' Alf.

methods. Alf has detected the source of recurring, long-term termite problems which, without his amazing scent-finding ability, may never have been found.

This is just one more story that reminds us of the many remarkable ways our furry friends help us greatly with their amazing senses.

The Cocker Spaniel

With a high degree of intelligence, the cocker spaniel is an active dog with speed and endurance—a sporting dog that loves to hunt. With a long coat and long, hairy, floppy ears, this dog needs maintenance involving regular grooming and clipping. The cocker spaniel comes in an array of colours such as black and tan, black, red, golden, blue, orange and lemon, liver, tan and tricolour.

Training is a must, as being a free-spirited breed, this little fellow will do its own thing if not given direction. They also love their food, so it is important to watch their diet. With its lively disposition, the cocker spaniel is a dog with a lot to offer the right owner.

Dogs on the Land

Dogs have been used for hundreds of years to help the farmer manage his stock. To this day, they hold an invaluable position on the farm both protecting and transporting, or droving herds from place to place under the stockman's direction.

One well-trained dog can take the place of two men or women, working cattle or sheep, making great savings for the property owner in wages, board and lodgings, not to mention the costs incurred on their particular method of transport, be it horses or motorbikes.

Sheep and cattle dogs are some of the most devoted and loyal dogs, with an innate aptitude for working with strict obedience.

With this canine advantage even large properties, thousands of hectares in area and containing hundreds of head of stock, can be worked by one person.

The relationship between a stockman and his dog is a close one. It is an association that they will both truly depend upon. The dog must be able to work as an extension of the trainer, moving as if by remote control. Commands are given by whistles, hand signals and voice to move the dog in the desired direction or to come and sit behind. Most of the commands involved in successful mustering or droving are built around the two basic commands of 'come' and 'sit'. Being able to rely on the dog to sit and stay, when commanded to do so, is very important in this type of work, that this behaviour is constantly reinforced throughout the dog's whole life. After using praise, patting and sometimes treats to teach the pup to sit in the first place, often an owner will not show their mature dog any of this type of attention until the dog is first told to sit, and he subserviently does so. Thus, obeying the command to sit is always associated with receiving pleasure, attention and being told he is a good dog.

A dog's skill in fetching and finding are also important in a working situation where a dog may be asked to bring a herd of stock to the stockman or to search for stock that may be out of sight.

Another amazing trait of these dogs is their stalking ability. You may have observed a cattle dog or border collie, at your local off-leash park, begin to 'round up' other dogs at play by using a stalking approach. A slow, steady, confident approach with the head held low and the eyes fixed with an intense gaze, is an action that will stop even the largest of cattle in its tracks. A dog successful in dominating an animal with this skill is said to have 'eye', and it proves to be a very powerful tool in controlling a herd.

In cases where a stockman needs to leave the mustered herd for a particular reason, or camp overnight, a well-trained dog may be trusted to mind the mob, unassisted. This is a big responsibility that a good dog will accept after careful training.

Kennels for these dogs can be the most amusing structures, many made with anything that happens to be lying around. Seeing the different varieties fashioned out of things such as tyres and car bonnets, would teach many a city dog owner just how little luxury a dog really needs to be comfortable.

One of the most simple and effective kennels is found at 'Poolbrook' station, Nullamanna, in New South Wales. It simply consists of a tractor tyre with a piece of corrugated iron arched over it for shelter. There are also several other kennels at 'Poolbrook'—one for each dog—each made out of different materials in all shapes and sizes. The dogs are usually chained to their individual kennel during the day, when they are not working or surveying the property with their owner, and are always chained at night.

In winter, the owners, Rod and Rai Schieb, throw straw into the kennels for warmth. Even then, Rod says that the dogs usually discard this straw and dig their own hole in the dirt to keep warm. This in a climate where the overnight winter temperature drops to below zero!

There are many stories told about these active dogs. Some are even celebrated in song and prose, forever belonging to Australia's rich country folklore. These are some of the most devoted and loyal dogs with an innate joy for working with strict obedience. When well-trained, they are an absolute asset to any stockman or woman.

Sheep and Cattle Dogs

The breeds used for this type of work are the Australian cattle dog, Australian kelpie, border collie and any crossbreed of these, sometimes with a small percentage of other breeds, such as the dingo, bull terrier, German shepherd, German collie or boxer. Both male and female dogs are commonly used. Through breeding, the natural predatory behaviour of the wolf has been developed to form five main working characteristics:

a) Herding—the inherent ability to gather, and keep stock together in a mob using speed and aggression where needed;

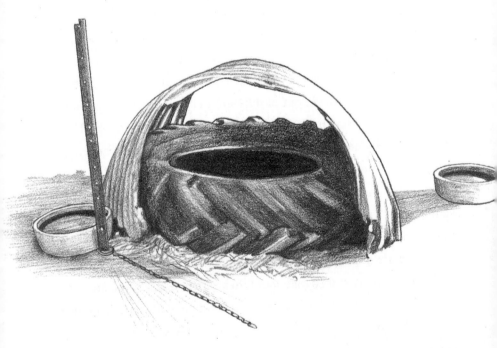

Kennels for sheep and cattle dogs can be the most amusing structures, many made with anything that happens to be lying around.

b) Heading—the ability to control the lead, or block with force, the head of the herd of stock;

c) Heeling (only for cattle)—the ability to bite or nip, hard and clean on the leg and sometimes the nose to control the herd by making the cattle submit to the dog's dominance;

d) Heeding—being obedient to the trainer's directions, understanding and taking them correctly; and

e) Hardiness—a strong, sound dog with endurance, speed and agility. Because they travel long distances, tough, deep padded feet are necessary.

Intelligence should be average to high. Very good dogs will be able to work independently, assessing constantly the changing situations put before them, and even occasionally going against the direction of their trainer to achieve a better outcome. Overall, these dogs are courageous and athletic—capable of quick and sudden movements. They are also known for their loyalty and protectiveness.

Born to be Legends

Traditionally, the Siberian Husky and Alaskan Malamute have been used as sled dogs in cold, icy regions. Sled dogs work together as a team, harnessed together usually in pairs of anything up to nine rows, to pull a carriage on skis. The weight of the cargo and/or passengers determines the number of dogs that need to be used for any particular trip. This team works as a pack, with their trainer a keen observer of the social interaction within this pack. The natural canine hierarchy is used to position the dogs on the sled, with the most dominant dog, or pair (equal to the alpha wolf) being placed as the leaders. However, the Top Dog of the sled pack is always the trainer, and this is constantly reinforced to the dogs through their training and throughout their whole working life.

Today, the Siberian husky and Alaskan Malamute are becoming increasingly popular in Australia, and clubs have been formed by the owners who wish to train, socialise and work their dogs. The fact that we don't have a lot of snow in Australia does not prevent enthusiasts from activities such as sled racing (in the forest), backpacking (bush walking trips where the dogs carry most of the supplies), and weight pulling contests, held during winter months when the temperature is below 15°C.

The husky and Malamute clubs, as with the clubs of other breeds, play an important role in educating owners about the breed, and in providing obedience training classes for their dogs. Anyone who owns one of these breeds will know they are strong-minded dogs that love to work—whether through training exercises or activities such as those mentioned above. The clubs recognise that the best way to control these dogs is to enable them to perform the work that they were designed to do. This has the added advantage of owners being able to interact with their dogs in an interesting, and often exhilarating, way.

The Siberian Husky

The Siberian husky is a working dog of medium size with a strong, well-balanced body for its natural role of hauling light loads at moderate speed over great distances. They can have brown or blue eyes, or even one of each. A friendly breed with an outgoing personality, the Siberian husky is a willing worker who is eager to please, given the right training and direction. Not a 'couch potato', this dog is born for action, so if you want to sit by your television all day, this is not the dog for you. However, if you are an active person who is prepared to spend plenty of time interacting with your dog, it will prove to be an excellent companion. Yes, the Siberian husky is most certainly active!

Originating from the north-east of Siberia (as their name suggests), the early inhabitants of this country, the Chukchi, relied on these dogs for survival. Huskies were almost worshipped by these people and played an important part in their religion. The Chukchi believed that if they were not caring of their dogs, they would not go to heaven. Breeding was selective, with only the lead dogs and those easy to train being free to mate (other dogs were tied up at mating times), thereby creating a strong, healthy breed. (This actually simulates the way the wolf breeds naturally in the wild, with the alpha wolves being the pair to breed, particularly in small packs). It was not until the early 20th century that the breed left its native land, first going to America, and then spreading via Alaska to many parts of the globe.

There are many stories that tell the heroic feasts of huskies. These dogs have incredible pulling skills which have been developed to transport both humans and their packages over treacherous, icy, snowy terrains using their senses and instincts to avoid the perils of thin ice, snowdrifts and deep crevices. Sometimes the distances travelled may be hundreds of kilometres away. In the cold, harsh north, many people have only survived because of the courage and tenacity of these sled dogs.

The Siberian husky has many stories of courage about its breed. The people of Nome, Alaska are eternally indebted to them for their courageous feat, carried out in 1925, when an epidemic of diptheria threatened to wipe out the whole town. Their supplies of antitoxin had run out and no suitable transport was available to bring the urgently needed serum some 1060 km to their town. It was the Siberian husky that responded to the call for help. Through the bleak winter snow and ice, the pride of the north came through, running in relay teams, day and night, to deliver the precious cargo to Nome. The whole journey was covered in an incredible five-and-a-half days. So impressed were the politicians of the day, that this life-saving expedition was recorded on their Congressional records.

The Alaskan Malamute

An attractive looking animal, the Alaskan Malamute has a strong, compact body with a deep chest and broad head, with brown almond-shaped eyes. It has a friendly disposition but, as with the husky, it requires strong leadership and lots of exercise.

This breed originated in north-western Alaska and owes its name to the Mahlemuts, the Inuit people who lived in this region. Before present-day transport, the Malamute was the freight dog of the Arctic. Its build enabled it to pull tremendous loads.

During the gold rush of 1896, the use of dog sleds increased and races were held to highlight their value. The heavy Malamute was not built for speed, and was therefore crossbred with a range of lighter and faster dogs. This has resulted in two different 'kinds' of Alaskan Malamutes. One line is called the M'Loot and the other is the Kotzebue. The main difference between these two blood lines is the size of the dog. M'Loot Malamutes are larger then the Kotzebues. True Kotzebues have only wolf-grey coats, whereas M'Loots come in a variety of colours, including wolf-grey, black and white, sable and

The sled team works as a pack and their natural canine hierarchy is used to position the dogs on the sled. However, the trainer is always the Top Dog.

white, seal, blue, and white. Although Kotzebues can be much more hyperactive than the M'Loot, they also tend to be less aggressive.

The male Malamute is 56 to 64 cm tall at the shoulder and weighs 29 to 39 kg; the female is 51 to 58 cm tall and weighs 23 to 32 kg. The dog has a woolly undercoat and a thick, coarse outer coat, and their appearance is wolf-like and dignified. They shed their undercoat completely twice a year in proportions as large as the dog itself.

Some owners describe their temperament like that of a child in the 'terrible two' stage. They are extremely intelligent, stubborn, headstrong, independent, easily bored and will constantly test their owner's authority. For this reason they are not recommended for first-time dog owners.

The Malamute remains a pack-oriented breed and is happiest when it is included with the family activities. It loves lots of attention.

6

Choosing the Best Friend for You

So, you've decided to buy a puppy. As you know, dogs come in all shapes and sizes—large, small, thin or stout. There are literally hundreds of different breeds of dogs and even more crossbreeds to choose from, so what should your choice be? Well, this depends on many factors, including where you live (in the country or the city), and the type of home you live in (a unit or a house).

For instance, working dogs such as cattle dogs, kelpies, border collies, German shepherds, Old English sheepdogs, Rottweilers and Dobermans all require lots of exercise and are probably better suited for country conditions rather than the city. However, if you have your heart set on one of these magnificent animals, then at least you should have a sizeable yard to accommodate such a pet.

If room is a problem (and you live in a unit or a house with a very small backyard) then maybe one of the toy breeds would be more suitable for you. These include Yorkshire terriers, silky terriers, poodles, miniature fox terriers, Maltese terriers, and King Charles spaniels.

The other part of the equation is the reason you have decided to purchase a puppy. Are you looking for a dog to provide protection or just wanting a friend and a companion to fill a need in your life? Naturally, the larger dogs are more usually suited to the role of watchdog, however the barking of a small dog will deter most people that may call unexpectedly.

If you are looking purely for a companion, then most breeds fill this criteria. It then simply comes down to an individual preference. The purchasing of a puppy is a serious decision and one that should always be taken with much thought and planning.

Buying a Puppy—Where and How?

Breeders

Excellent puppies can be purchased from dog breeding kennels in many areas. These breeders, in most cases, have a very professional attitude about the dogs they are breeding and with their vast experience, will often help you on the road to choosing a puppy suitable for you. Many buyers who purchase from kennels do so because they intend to show their puppy in show trials, and kennels often breed from parents who have already excelled in this way.

Pet Shops

Your local pet shop is another fine source for acquiring your puppy. Pet shops are normally located in convenient areas such as your local shopping centre. You will find the puppies are well cared for and you will have a large choice of various breeds in one easy to reach location.

Many of these puppies are pure bred, however, if you wish to purchase a less expensive puppy, most pet shops have mixed breed puppies at a lower price.

If the particular puppy that you wish to purchase is not available, some pet shops will buy it in for you at your request.

The cost varies, but most pet shops are competitive with their prices. Pet shops also make it a habit to have the puppies checked out by their local veterinarian, ensuring that you take home a healthy and happy puppy.

Newspapers

Your metropolitan and local newspaper is another avenue open to you when purchasing your new puppy. Through these media you are often able to acquire a good pet at the right price, but as with any purchase, one must take care, as you do not have the same recourse when dealing with a private source as you would with pet shops and kennels. However, having said that, many excellent small breeders regularly sell their puppies in this way and have been able to satisfy a lot of happy owners.

Animal Welfare Shelters

The RSPCA is well known as being a place for purchasing a puppy in need of a good home at a nominal cost. Inoculations, worming, etc. are usually included in the price.

There are other animal shelters which operate in much the same way and do a marvellous job at caring for abandoned and unwanted animals. Puppies and dogs can be acquired at reasonable prices from these organisations.

What do I Watch Out For?

When buying a puppy it should already have been weaned. This normally takes place at around six weeks of age and the puppy is usually ready to go home with you at approximately eight weeks.

In many cases your puppy will have had its first inoculation from the vet and will have been wormed, which is necessary at about this age. The puppy will require another inoculation approximately six weeks later, plus worming.

You should examine the puppy thoroughly for any abnormalities and signs of possible sickness. A good sign of a healthy puppy is usually a lively temperament, clear eyes, no odour in the ears or bad breath, and a normal size tail for its body size. In some larger breeds, problems with hip displacement can occur. If you are concerned in any way, a check of your new puppy by your local vet will allay any fears.

The First Night

A little planning on the first night you bring your puppy home can help to alleviate a most troublesome time. Firstly, make sure that the location you intend to keep your puppy in for the first few weeks is safe and your puppy is not in danger of falling, which may cause dislocation or breakage of bones at such a fragile age. A cardboard box with high sides and an old blanket, or something similar, would be suitable. I have also found in my experience that an old wind-up clock with a distinct ticking sound or a radio turned down low will often calm a puppy that is missing its mother and siblings. If you purchase the puppy in winter, a hot water bottle can also be a marvellous way to settle your puppy down for the first night.

Puppies at this age need to go to the toilet on a regular basis, so you need to take the puppy outside frequently or supply paper for it to use to go to the toilet if left inside.

A suitable first night bed for a puppy need only be a cardboard box with high sides and an old blanket.

Toilet Training

I am often called by clients who are almost in despair because they have been unable to train their dog to a satisfactory stage of toilet training. Some of these clients have dogs six and seven months old that still refuse to go to the toilet in a designated place. So let's look at the basics of toilet training.

There are two main times when a dog will want to go to the toilet—after it has eaten and when it wakes up from a sleep. The next part of the equation is that dogs instinctively look for a porous surface to go to the toilet, such as mats, timber, sand, soil, and grass. Dogs usually won't go to the toilet on nonporous surfaces such as linoleum, tiles, and metal.

Another factor is that dogs usually won't go to the toilet near their food, water or bed, so to toilet train your dog you need to use a room such as a bathroom or a laundry with a nonporous floor, such as tiles or linoleum.

Choose the room most suitable for you to start to toilet train your pup. You will need to put a generous amount of newspaper into this room, sufficient to enable your dog to go to the toilet. Do not put food into this room. When the puppy has been fed, and after sleeping, put it in there and leave it until it goes to the toilet, which you will find it will soon get into the habit of doing. If you have a piece of the dog dropping to place on the paper, this will enhance the procedure. There are also drops available on the market that you can acquire from your local pet shop, that will encourage your puppy to go to the toilet. Keep this method up for two weeks, then simply leave this room available with paper, the door open and the puppy should go there on its own as it has become accustomed to doing. You should always try to catch the puppy in the act of going to the toilet in the correct place and praise it. If your dog makes an accident, then just ignore it.

If you want your puppy to go to the toilet outside, the paper can be moved firstly to the entrance to the outside door and then eventually, outside. This will encourage your puppy to go to the door and let you know when it wants to relieve itself.

How Puppies Think and Act

If you had wanted to acquire a puppy a thousand years ago, chances are you would have had to go out into the wild, because that is where the dogs were as wolves. In their natural state dogs are pack animals with the leader being the most fierce and dominant dog in the pack. Every other dog has a pecking order from the strongest at the top of the pack, down to the very frail dogs at the bottom. It is instinctive for each dog to want to be the leader of the pack or as high up in the pecking order as possible and the only way they can do this is by being more aggressive than the dog above them.

Now, in modern times, when we purchase a puppy and bring that puppy home, it's essential that we remember that its instincts are the same as they were many years ago—your little puppy wants to be the leader of the pack. As far as the puppy is concerned, the new family now becomes its pack and it wants to be Top Dog. So to have a dog that you are in control of and therefore, the master of, you need to assume the position of Top Dog with your puppy from the very beginning.

Temperament

Dogs, like people, all have different temperaments. Some of that temperament has been passed down genetically, whereas other parts have been developed because of the dog's environment. This is why it is very important how we handle our pet at the puppy stage. A puppy that is mishandled, and that is not taught good manners, can develop bad habits that will stay with it throughout its life. So, let's look at the different types of temperaments that dogs have.

Overly Timid Dogs

A dog can become overly suspicious and frightened of strangers because it has not been socialised at an early age. So, encourage friends and relatives to handle your new puppy and for them to play with it and pet it gently. Children should also be encouraged to be gentle with the new family pet. A new puppy should be socialised at every opportunity, as only then will this type of temperament in a dog dissipate.

Aggressive Dogs

As friendly and loving as most dogs may be, it has been my experience that most dogs will bite if put under extreme circumstances. A dog that bites at will has usually inherited this in its genes or has been mishandled at one time or another. This mishandling mainly happens when the dog is in its puppy stage.

You will often find a puppy using its teeth to mouth you in play and most people take this as simply being a thing that puppies do. This behaviour, in actual fact, is the puppy being dominant and showing dominance over another puppy (as it sees you). Because dogs don't realise that we are humans, they just feel that we are part of their pack and they put each and every one of us in a pecking order, as they would have naturally in a pack situation. If we are not able to take a dominant role, that of Top Dog, an aggressive dog will automatically want to be above us in the pecking order and use aggressive behaviour, including biting, to achieve this aim. So, here we need to assert our authority and be more dominant where needs be, but also kind and just. Only then will a dog respect us and obey our wishes.

Anything connected with using teeth by a dog is a sign of dominance and may eventually lead to a dog biting, so if your puppy mouths you, reprimand it with an 'Aah aah'.

Environment

In this world of ours we have many different environments, and these diversities can have huge effects on our dog's behaviour. In some parts of the world dogs have not traditionally been a part of the culture of that country, resulting in thousands of stray dogs roaming the streets, scavenging for food where they can. Over the years, I have visited some of these places. It's hard to describe it, but these dogs look nothing like dogs I see on a day-to-day basis in Australia. I found these dogs to be very aloof and, although not aggressive, they were not friendly either. In some instances, I tried to call a few of them to me but the effort was in vain. I think their daily struggle with life had a huge bearing on their behaviour, determined by their environment.

I've often seen owners with small yards who own large dogs like German shepherds that are not walked regularly. These dogs can chase and bite their tail until it bleeds. This, I believe, is due to the stress of being locked in a small yard without regular exercise because the owner was tired of being pulled down the road by an untrained dog.

It is said that we should not argue in front of our children as it is bad for them, but rarely do we give our dog the same courtesy. An environment where the family is arguing is not conducive to having a well-adjusted and happy dog. Arguing disturbs a dog because it sees the family as its pack and arguing as aggression. Instead of enjoying the unity wolves have available to them in a pack situation, there is conflict. This is disturbing for a dog. It is imperative that an owner understands that the dog's environment greatly affects its behaviour and a good environment is vital to curing a dog's behavioural problems.

Most bad behaviour comes mainly from either our interaction with our dog or the environment. There are other components which have a bearing on behaviour such as genetics, diet, hormones, de-sexing, etc., but in my experience, a dog's environment and our interaction with it has the most impact.

Enriching your dog's environment can greatly help in improving its behaviour and this may be achieved by doing some quite simple things. Let's start with the backyard. In many cases, a backyard is the place in which a dog spends a considerable amount of time. The following ideas can help entertain your dog in your backyard:

a) A sandpit can be an excellent playing area for your dog. All that is required is to dig out an area of about 1 m² x 60–80 cm deep in the back of your yard and fill it with sand. Tie up your dog nearby as you bury its favourite toy. It will soon get the idea and all you need do after that is to keep burying as many toys as possible, to give him a good play pen.

b) Hanging toys are also excellent amusers. Toys in which you are able to insert food are great for hanging from fences or trees. Try attaching them in such a way that they will swing when your dog is trying to get the food out. Peanut butter, cream cheese or something similar is a good filler, and you should pack it well inside to make it hard for your dog to get out, so it is kept entertained for some time and distracted from displacement activities such as digging and chewing. There are also plenty of dog toys and play things to keep your dog busy and amused. We just need to do a little lateral thinking.

c) Plastic bottles filled with meaty flavoured gravy, punctured with just one or two tiny pinholes, is another play toy you can make yourself and one which is a great attention holder for many dogs.

As I mentioned previously, dogs need to be walked. They need the exercise it gives, but even more than that, they need the natural adventure of a walk, which they miss by not going hunting, as they would have done, regularly, in their natural life in the wild as the wolf. As we know, there is little exercise or adventure in the way we now feed our domestic dogs. Their food mainly comes out of a packet, or a tin is simply opened and the food placed in their bowl. Dog's food is given to them on a platter! The only hunting stimulation dogs usually get these days is their walk, so making time for it is a must. Your dog should be walked at least once a day and my opinion is that it needs to be of at least twenty to thirty minutes duration. If your dog has arthritis or another similar ailment, you should speak to your vet about alternatives.

Another wolf instinct that is still strong in most of our dogs is that of the chase. The wolf's skills in chase have to be practiced and fine-tuned in the wild, or the catching of food would be sparse. Yes, the instinct to chase is still very prominent in many of our dogs and, of course, has been selectively bred in many of them. This natural behaviour can be utilised to our advantage by simply taking along a ball to our local off-leash park to throw for our dog. Here we can throw the ball, or hit the ball with a tennis racquet (for long range runners), until it wants to chase it no longer. With some doggies, that can take a long, long time! Even so, this little exercise can result in a dog that only wants to rest when he gets home and with some clients that I know, this situation would be heaven.

I also find long bush walks excellent adventures that you can share with your dog. There is an area not far away from where I live where owners can throw sticks or balls into the water for their dogs to retrieve. This is a wonderful exercise and very stimulating for both dog and owner.

However, I offer a word of caution where sticks are involved: sticks are liable to break, leaving jagged ends that can be dangerous. When thrown, they can flick up, piercing the chest or underbelly of your dog. Many nasty accidents have been caused in this way. For this reason, I suggest you use something other than a stick.

Encouraging your dog to retrieve in the water can be a very exciting, pleasant game, especially on a hot summer's day.

Put your doggie hat on and think. There are an enormous amount of games, excursions, toys, and play things which you can use to enrich your dog's life and give you both enjoyable experiences leading to a closer companionship. Sometimes when this happens, it is very easy to believe that you and your dog know exactly what each other is thinking.

The Need to Socialise

The socialisation of a dog forms the very foundation of its behaviour. Lack of socialising can result in aggression against humans, inter-dog aggression, fear biting or even a frightened dog that is afraid of the slightest noise or movement. These and many other behavioural problems can be avoided with effective socialising.

Start Young

All dogs, no matter what the breed, need socialising and the earlier you start—the better. Your puppy should come home with you at eight weeks of age, however, things do not always work out this way. So, no matter how old your dog, start to socialise it as soon as possible. Contrary to popular belief, dogs do not arrive on this planet automatically able to associate with people or other dogs. Nor are they familiar with worldly sounds that we take for granted.

Dogs need to be socialised with humans, as well as other dogs, from an early age, to prevent them from becoming aggressive (a situation which can create enormous problems as the dog matures). Survival is one of the most powerful instincts in all creatures, and dogs are no exception. This instinct is what drives our dog to be suspicious of anything strange to it. Sometimes, when a dog confronts something outside of its experience that frightens it, its instinctive flight, fright or freeze mode comes into play. This is why a noisy skateboard that unexpectedly comes toward your dog, frightening it, can turn it either into an aggressive dog, or one that will shy away from the foreign object, as its survival instincts take over. Its reaction will depend on how well it has been familiarised with this type of situation.

If possible, take your pup to puppy school. Here it will have the opportunity to interact with other dogs of all shapes and sizes. This is an important part of your dog's development. Often a dog can become comfortable with its own breed, obviously because of its interaction with siblings and its mother from birth, but may be aggressive with other breeds if not given the opportunity to meet and play with them.

Plenty of human socialising is also important. This can be achieved by allowing friends to gently play with your puppy when they call upon you. However, if the puppy is shy, never let anyone force themselves on your puppy. Always let the puppy accept humans or dogs that are strange to it at its own pace—never hurry it.

Many times I have called on a client that has a dog that goes totally out of control every time they start up the mower or vacuum cleaner, barking and biting at it furiously. This would never have occurred if the dog had been familiarised with these types of sounds as a puppy. Refer to page 85 for tips on how to fix this problem.

It is important to introduce your dog to crowded places, busy traffic, water, and as many strange places and sounds as possible. Success with socialising comes with one essential ingredient—patience. Be like Napoleon, who would say to his driver, 'Go slowly, I'm in a hurry'.

Diet

Opinions of what we should feed our dog are varied, depending on the source of the dietary information and whether there is a conflict of interest at play. I, personally feel that, as with so many things in life, there is no right answer to this, as all dogs are individuals, with different metabolisms, different genetics and different breeding.

Each stage a dog goes through, be it pregnancy, puppydom, adulthood or old age, requires particular nutritional needs. Working dogs also have special dietary needs compared with a pet dog that sleeps all day and goes out for a walk occasionally. What is a balanced diet for one group of dogs may not necessarily be suitable for another.

If we understand the nutritional requirements of our dogs, we have a better chance of getting it right, and this then gives our dog the optimum chance to develop to its full potential. So let's start with the basics. There are six major nutrients—water, protein, carbohydrates, fats, minerals and vitamins—and dogs need these for good health.

Water

Dogs need clean drinking water at all times. Water has many functions in the body—it breaks down nutrients so that they can be transported through the dog's system for digestive purposes, it moves nutrients around the body, it regulates body temperature and eliminates food waste. Good drinking water is vital for our dog's wellbeing.

Protein

Dogs need high-quality protein, as this is an important building block of their body. Protein breaks down into amino acids, which are the body's main material for tissue building and maintenance and help the neurotransmitter activity of the dog's brain. Sources of protein include soya, and meats such as chicken, lamb, kangaroo and beef.

Carbohydrates

The activity levels of dogs are different, as are their energy needs, but no matter what their requirements, carbohydrates give them instant energy. Carbohydrates are the body's preferred fuel and are derived from such foods as bread, rice, pasta, wheat and other grain products.

Fats

Fats are needed in a dog's diet to supply essential fatty acids and to transport the vitamins, A, D, E and K, throughout the body—so we should never put our dog on a fat-free diet. Fatty acids also promote a shiny coat. Fatty acids are found in beef, pork, lamb, fish, olive oil, some vegetables and almonds.

Minerals

All dogs require minerals. An array of minerals, such as phosphorous and calcium is needed for many body functions, including keeping the dog's bones and teeth healthy. Other minerals, including magnesium, chloride, potassium, sodium and trace elements, such as copper, iodine, zinc and iron, are all necessary for a well-balanced diet. Sources of minerals come from all the major food groups including dairy products, fish, nuts and vegetables, meat and poultry.

Vitamins

Vitamins are essential for dogs. Vitamins are numerous and have many functions. There are two groups of vitamins—water-soluble and fat-soluble. Fat-soluble vitamins stay in the body longer. Vitamin A, known as 'visual purple', is needed to aid visual sensations. It also assists in building bones and promotes healthy skin and protects the mucus linings of the respiratory and digestive tracts. Vitamin B has many variants that include riboflavin, niacin and folate. They all are necessary for good vision, rejuvenation of cells and maintenance of the nervous system. Vitamin C is an antioxidant which helps build the immune system and is also essential for bone growth. Vitamin D comes from the sun and helps the body absorb calcium which is beneficial to bone growth, and finally vitamin E which destroys free radicals and also assists the immune system. Sources of vitamins include vegetables, eggs, fish, grains and meat.

What to Feed your Dog

Most dogs will eat an array of different foods, however I find the average person is in a quandary as to what to feed their dog. Put simply, there are probably two main methods of feeding our dog—the 'owner-prepared' method and the 'commercial' method. It is simply up to the individual and their lifestyle as to which method they choose.

The 'owner-prepared' method is a diet consisting of foods, such as meat, grains, rice, pasta, dairy products and vegetables. We can also feed our dog a balanced commercial food diet (dry dog food or canned food) which contains all the necessary nutrients, including proteins, carbohydrates, fats, minerals and vitamins.

How Much to Feed your Dog

The following is a suggested program to feed your dog. No one but you, or your vet, can really decide on the right amount of food for your dog. Young puppies need small, regular meals and the food should be moist. This ensures that their food is digested and that they are getting the necessary nutrients they need at this crucial age. Four meals a day is usually recommended for puppies eight to twelve weeks old; at twelve to sixteen weeks only three meals a day is required. Over sixteen weeks progress to two meals a day. If more suitable to your dog and your lifestyle, you may feed your dog once a day when it reaches adulthood.

Home prepared meals

Home prepared meals should consist of meat, mixed cereal, mixed vegetables, vegetable oils plus supplements of vitamins and minerals. Puppies can be fed 70 per cent raw minced meat, 20 per cent mixed grains (often rolled oats or whole grain oats which have been soaked overnight) and steamed rice, plus 10 per cent lightly cooked mixed vegetables, vegetable oils and supplements of multivitamins and minerals. Add to that a raw bone every two or three days (usually a knucklebone or mutton flaps) and lots of clean water. As puppies grow, you can reduce the meat content to about 48–50 per cent and increase the grain and vegetable content.

Commercial food

It is best to feed your dog premium commercial food brands. These products have a complete and balanced diet and there is an array of different types to satisfy any dog's nutritional requirements without having to add anything other than a raw bone. An added advantage is that the manufacturer stipulates the amount of food to give your dog depending on its weight and size.

The amount to feed your dog will always depend on variables such as its breed, size, metabolism and activity levels. Climate should also be taken into consideration. Of course, one of the best ways of finding out if you are feeding your dog correctly is by keeping an eye on its weight and discussing any sudden fluctuations with your vet.

Lifestyle

The life we lead has a great influence on our dog's behaviour and likewise, our dog's behaviour has a great influence on our quality of life. A person who works from home may have their dog by their side all day and this can be pleasant for both dog and owner. Strong bonding can occur. However, I have also seen this create huge problems when the owner needs to leave the home.

A dog whose favourite pack member is its constant companion, can feel abandoned when left at home while that pack member goes out 'hunting' (for example shopping), and will often suffer from behavioural problems such as separation anxiety (as covered in chapter three). This can bring with it chronic bouts of chewing, hole digging and frantic efforts to escape the property by scratching and pulling furiously at fences and gates, or continuous barking.

Owners sometimes try to stop this behaviour by locking dogs in the house whilst they are out, only to return to find their house wrecked. One such lady recently told me about her dog that had totally destroyed the expensive lounge suite she had just purchased, by tearing all the lining up and chewing the wooden legs. This dog was almost sent off to the local dog shelter.

We do need to bond with our dog, but over-bonding, because of our particular lifestyle, can be a huge mistake.

The direct opposite situation can also be a problem whereby people, because of work or other commitments, have no choice but to leave their dog on its own for long periods. The dog, being a social animal, cannot cope with this isolation. I know of owners who work long hours, sometimes being away from home from 7am until 8 or

9pm, leaving their dog on its own. They then wonder why their dog is having behavioural problems. If this is your lifestyle, you may need to consider organising for your dog to be walked during the day by a friend or family member. Alternatively, there are now day-care centres in some areas where your dog can go and have the company of other dogs while you are busy with your routine. Your dog needs interaction with you on a regular basis and a dog that is trained and walked daily is a dog with less problems.

The above ideas, and those given previously under the 'Environment' heading, are just a few suggestions. I'm sure you would be able to add to these with just a bit of thought on your part, to come up with some activities to suit your own situation and circumstance.

Owning a dog is a huge responsibility. One that cannot be taken lightly, and I feel anyone contemplating acquiring a dog must first take their lifestyle into consideration, before deciding on the type of dog they would be able to manage. Our dogs need lots of care and attention and this takes time, effort and commitment on our part.

As I conclude, may I leave you with this brief but very important message—be dominant and assertive with your dog when the need arises, but remember, do not bully or shout at your dog, as this will always have disastrous results. To form a good human/canine relationship you need to be both dominant and kind (which you should now understand, having read this book). Then all you will have to do to control your dog is just whisper.

Index